Developing

MAKING ORGANIZATIONS MORE HUMAN ⎯⎯⎯⎯⎯⎯⎯

The Curious Organization

Cutting-edge thinking to catalyze your leadership practice

Publisher's note

Every effort has been made to ensure information contained in this publication is accurate at the time of going to press. Neither the publishers nor any of the contributors can accept responsibility for any errors or omissions, however caused, nor for any loss or damage occasioned to any person acting, or refraining from action, as a result of the material in this publication.

Users and readers of this publication may copy portions of the material for personal use, internal reports, or reports to clients provided that such articles (or portions of articles) are attributed to this publication by name, the individual contributor of the portion uses and publisher, **IdeasforLeaders.com**.

IEDP Ideas for Leaders Ltd
42 Moray Place, Edinburgh, EH3 6BT

Copyright ©2022 IEDP Ideas for Leaders Ltd and contributors

Publishers: Roland Deiser and Roddy Millar
Editor-in-Chief: Roddy Millar
Associate Editors: Saar Ben-Attar (Africa); Conrado Schlochauer (LatAm);
                       Ravi Shankar (SE Asia)
Art Direction: Nick Mortimer – nickmortimer.co.uk

Printed by Lightning Source

www.developingleadersquarterly.com
www.ideasforleaders.com
www.futureorg.org

ISBN 978-1-91-552905-3

Contents

Editor's Letter: Roddy Millar

C uriosity is the theme of this issue, but it is really the theme of all our issues. We are led by curiosity here at DLQ. It is what takes us to new places to find new ideas and leads us to understand how emerging thinking fits with, replaces or invigorates current processes.

Curiosity comes in lots of shapes and sizes – we understood this better when thinking about the graphics to use in this issue. Some people get drawn into the minutiae of things (the microscope), others are drawn to looking over the horizon (the telescope); others still are intrigued by how things fit together (dismantling the clock) and then there is curiosity over emotions and human interactions. What is also clear is that for many, our curiosity and sense of inquiry is diluted and frequently extinguished by years of formulaic education and strict business process.

In this issue we have three articles that focus on curiosity – Simon Brown is interviewed by my co-publisher, Roland Deiser. Simon is Chief Learning Officer at the global pharma giant, Novartis, and co-author of *The Curious Advantage*, and he brings insight into how Novartis has fostered a curious mindset in its employees. Stefaan van Hooydonk, Director of the Global Curiosity Institute, gives a broader overview of the impact that curious organization can generate; and our Africa editor, Saar Ben-Attar, profiles the hugely successful South African businessman, Mxolisi Mgojo, who has put curiosity at the centre of his career success.

We are also running a roundtable on curiosity on November 3rd, with Simon Brown and Saar Ben-Attar plus star Harvard faculty, Prof Francesca Gino and Dr Perry Zurn, who has just published *Curious Minds* (reviewed in this issue) with his twin sibling, Dani Bassett. Do be sure to register for that session on the link at the foot of this letter.

This issue is our second in our new pocket-sized format, and we continue to receive excited feedback for this new design. Our primary objective with it though, is to get readers to create that precious space to 'stop and reflect' on their own leadership practice – this is the first, and most important step on all our leadership journeys, and we strongly believe that you will gain far more impact by doing that reading away from a screen. We all stare at screens too much and for too long – and we know that quiet reflection cannot really happen while we do so. Our mind cannot reach that sense of calm while notifications ping and links take our curious minds down rabbit-holes. To truly get a bit of the necessary space to think we need to find some peace and we hope that dipping into the print issue of DLQ will both catalyse your thinking and foster some moments of reflection on your own leadership practice. And at our current print copy low price it is much cheaper and longer lasting than attending a leadership program!

Elsewhere in this issue we bring you our usual eclectic range of insights and research. Bay Jordan asks the powerful question 'if people are our greatest asset, why do they not appear on the balance sheet as assets?' – and explores the negative implications that that creates. Henrik Cronqvist and Desiree-Jessica Pely share how CEOs backgrounds and personal life experiences shape their management styles. Donna Kennedy-Glans and James Kerr discuss Vision Statements as a way for organizations to navigate stormy political questions. Wendy Shepherd shares her research on why executive development so often fails to deliver – and what we can do to prevent that. Paul Brown shines his light on how emotions really direct all that we do. Plus some Ideas from Ideas for Leaders and our book reviews – there is a lot to digest here – take you time, dip in and out, and enjoy!

Have a great autumn/fall wherever you are – and stay curious!

Roddy Millar | Editor-in-Chief

As ever, if you have any stories you would like to share with us for potential pieces in the magazine or for discussion on the DLQ website, please let me know at **editor@ideasforleaders.com**.

Register for our Curiosity Roundtable (November 3, 2022)
us02web.zoom.us/webinar/register/
WN_f55kVQufTjiNNcYAX2Iskw

Subscribe to DLQ Print issues
developingleadersquarterly.com/subscribe/

Roland Deiser in conversation
with Novartis' CLO Simon Brown

Building a Curious Organization

"An organization that nurtures curiosity provides you with a toolset that enables you to navigate through uncertainty and ambiguity." —Simon Brown

Roland Deiser

Simon, you co-authored the book, The Curious Advantage. What made you write this book?

Simon Brown

Well, in spring 2019, in the space of a couple of weeks, two people completely independently said to me 'You should write a book about what you're doing at Novartis.' It was strange, because I never thought about writing a book, and I had no idea what it would take. Soon after I was having dinner with Paul Ashcroft and Garrick Jones and was picking their brains as

I focused first and foremost on the curiosity dimension, as it has a clear relationship to a learning culture

they had written a book previously. As they had been involved in the Novartis journey from very early on, we decided we would write a book together on Curiosity. They also had their own take on curiosity and were able to bring their own experiences and ideas. So we agreed we would do it as the three of us, which I think was a great move, because the social commitment of doing it together made us move more rapidly through the process.

RD We know that when your CEO took on the role at Novartis, he wanted to transform the culture of the company by driving three core values across the organization: Inspired, curious, and unbossed. Why is curiosity among those three? There could be many others, such as agility, creativity, customer focus, and so on. Why curiosity?

SB Well, the three values were building on Dan Pink's research that identified autonomy, mastery and purpose as key drivers of what motivates us. Autonomy translated then into unbossed, purpose into inspired, and mastery into curiosity. In my role as Chief Learning Officer, I focused first and foremost on the curiosity dimension, as it has a clear relationship to a learning culture. But curiosity was also interesting to me because I saw

Simon Brown, CLO, Novartis

it as a meta-skill that not only powers learning but reaches way beyond. When we started out, not many people were talking about it like that. Curiosity in a corporate setting was relatively new, and we felt it could become a major catalyst for cultural transformation.

RD So, how do you see the importance of curiosity beyond its traditional role as a driver for learning?

SB I see curiosity as the greatest driver of value in the digital age, and this is the premise of the book. The world is getting more ambiguous, things are exponentially getting faster, we face uncharted territory. How do you navigate through such a world when textbook solutions are no longer valid? Being curious provides a way to navigate through that uncertainty. Curiosity is about wondering, it is about coming up with ideas, questions, and then exploring those questions to test out what works, what doesn't work, and then learning from the results. An organization that nurtures curiosity provides you with a toolset that enables you to navigate through uncertainty and ambiguity.

RD So how do you then start out to create a culture of curiosity?

SB Firstly it is worth being very clear that changing a company culture is hard, and takes a long time! Leader role modeling was absolutely key: leaders talking about curiosity, leaders sharing what they were learning, and creating and sharing playlists about the learning that they were doing. We used symbols and campaigns, such as a curiosity month, a whole month dedicated to being curious and we had a number of learning interventions that showed the importance we were placing on curiosity. We provided access to great new learning resources, such as to Coursera and LinkedIn Learning. We started talking about an aspiration that people would invest 5% of their time to building new skills and knowledge, and being curious. So there were many different aspects - access to learning, leadership role modeling, campaigns and promotions related to learning and curiosity, and more. All these elements supported that culture change, but it is a journey we are still on.

Organizational Curiosity

A CFFO/DLQ Virtual Round Table

Curiosity drives creativity and innovation, creates connectivity, and fosters cross-boundary collaboration – key ingredients organizations need in times of digital transformation and ecosystem-based value creation.

Simon Brown
Chief Learning Officer
Co-Author of *The Curious Advantage* | Novartis

Francesca Gino
Professor of Business Administration | Author of *Rebel Talent* | Harvard Business School

Perry Zurn
Professor of Philosophy
Co-Author of *Curious Minds*
American University

Saar Ben-Attar
Managing Director, Ascent Growth Partners | Executive Fellow, CFFO

Roland Deiser (Host)
Founder and Chairman, Center for the Future of Organization

PRACTICE LEADERSHIP MEETS THOUGHT LEADERSHIP

Connecting perspectives from Academia, Business, and Consulting (ABC), our roundtables bring together the world's most prominent thought and practice leaders of this space to engage in an unscripted dialogue on the subject.

NOVEMBER 3, 2022 | 11:00-12:30 ET   **REGISTER FREE**

CFFO CENTER FOR THE FUTURE OF ORGANIZATION | DRUCKER SCHOOL OF MANAGEMENT Claremont Graduate University

DevelopingLeaders Quarterly

> *People struggled with what we meant by curiosity. What does it look like? What does it mean? What do I have to do differently?*

RD And did people pick up on that easily? Or was it kind of an uphill battle to promote curiosity?

SB It's interesting. I remember that initially people struggled with what we meant by curiosity. What actually does curiosity look like? What does it actually mean? What do I have to do differently? That that was when we stepped in with a lot of the campaigns and pieces I just talked about. And it worked. If we look at metrics, data tells a good story. In 2018, before we started the journey, we'd had 22.6 hours as our average amount of learning per person across the company. Fast forward three years to 2021, we were on 52.1 hours.

RD What counts in this metric as learning?

SB It's a mix. We have our major learning systems, but we also recognize that a lot of learning happens uncaptured by those systems, more informal learning. So we provided a mechanism for people to be able to track their learning through an app. If I was attending a conference, I could add that time in my learning hours. Or if I'm having a conversation with a colleague over lunch and they're explaining what their part of the organization is and I'm learning about that, I can track that time as learning time.

1. CONTEXT – *Explore broadly*

The broader the context you expose yourself to, the more likely you will find new ideas that stimulate you to explore further.

2. COMMUNITY – *Connect with a diverse group*

Curiosity is powered by our community. Societies or organizations with curiosity as a specific part of culture are more productive and people are more engaged in learning and in their work.

3. CURATION – *Edit and focus*

Curiosity is powered by our community. Societies or organizations with curiosity as a specific part of culture are more productive and people are more engaged in learning and in their work.

4. CREATIVITY
– Do something deliberately differently

Our exploration into new worlds may require us to think differently, connect something in a new way and make a leap of faith. Sometimes, it's the spark that starts a new cycle of curiosity.

5. CONSTRUCTION – *Try things out in the real world*

Curiosity is not just wondering. It is putting you wonder into action. This means making or constructing something to learn about it. Whether it's making new connections, building something physical, writing a document, a piece of music, building a business or just figuring out how something works..

6. CRITICALITY – *Check your biases*

Asking questions is deeply connected to being curious. It is the questions that prompt us to discover and find solutions. The type of questions we apply are important if we want to know if there is a different or better way. We also need to be aware of our own biases.

7. CONFIDENCE
– Build in little 'failures' to grow in confidence

Asking questions is deeply connected to being curious. It is the questions that prompt us to discover and find solutions. The type of questions we apply are important if we want to know if there is a different or better way. We also need to be aware of our own biases.

RD I see. But I think there remains still a lot of learning that may not show up in your system. Each encounter with a customer - or any stakeholder for that matter - becomes a learning experience if done with a curious attitude. I guess my question is: Do you have elements in your learning architecture that institutionalize curiosity on an organizational level, through policies or other mechanisms?

SB We try to institutionalize a culture of curiosity through various systemic elements. For example, we rolled out a program for all of our leaders to enable them to become an unbossed leader. We know that a leader can make or break curiosity within a team, and unbossed leadership plays a major role. That included creating psychological safety in teams, a safe space where people can ask questions, can experiment, can fail and then learn from those failures – this is how we achieve innovation. Scaling this across the organization was a systematic way to make sure to create an environment in which people could be curious.

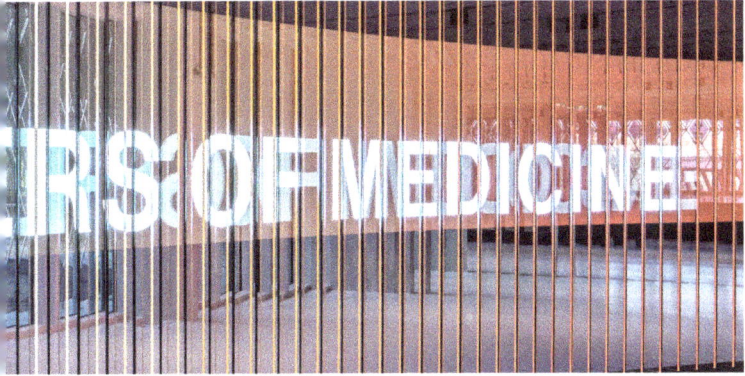

RD One way to look at curiosity is that it's a driver for reaching out beyond your horizon and making new connections. Are you curious beyond your area of expertise, i.e. do you want to learn about and connect with other industries, other functions, other businesses? Or does your curiosity remain within the silo of your professional knowledge domain? Do you address this angle of curiosity in any way?

SB In our book, we have the Seven Cs model for curiosity, and one of the dimensions is community. We argue that being curious is best not done alone; you need to find a community. There are many different roles within a community of people who can be curious with you and travel on that journey. There are people who can unlock information for you - sort of gatekeepers to new information and new communities and new areas. There are people who have the wisdom of having done it before, and they can share that wisdom in whatever it is that you're curious about. So there's a whole portfolio of different roles that can help in being curious. Identifying those and finding

Applying this insight in a corporate context means that curiosity works against being siloed...

who's going to be helpful on that journey is a key part. Applying this insight in a corporate context means that curiosity works against being siloed in one's own areas.

RD Can you talk a bit more about the Seven Cs that drive curiosity?

SB Sure. So, the seven are context, community, curation, creativity, construction, criticality and confidence. *Context* means to explore broadly, to move beyond your boundaries. The broader the context you expose yourself to, the more likely you will find ideas that stimulate you to explore further.

Community – we just talked about this. It's about connecting with a diverse group that provides access to rich resources. Diversity is important here. Then – *Curation*, which is about making choices. We must intentionally curate our curiosity to synthesize and focus our thinking, our ideas, and the information we are gathering.

Next is *Creativity*, which is about doing something deliberately in a different way, asking new questions and exploring new ideas. How can we connect something that seems unrelated? Thinking about different worlds often creates a spark that starts a new cycle of curiosity. Then there is *Construction*, which means you must go beyond thinking and try things out on the real world. Curiosity is not just wondering. It is putting your wonder into action. Whether it's making new connections,

Frank Gehry building, Novartis campus, Basel

building something physical, writing a document, or just figuring out how something works.

After construction comes *Criticality*. Criticality is about applying a critical lens to the results of our construction, to our experiments. We also must be critical against ourselves by questioning our own biases.

And finally, *Confidence* – something that grows if we are curious. The two actually grow with each other. If we approach something new with a curious mindset, being open to trying, failing and improving – we build our confidence, which in turn encourages us to be even more curious.

By following these seven C you can target one's curiosity, rather than being aimless and sort of drifting around. We cover this in our book in a lot more detail and share examples how we use that within a company to foster a culture of curiosity.

Novartis Pavillion, Basel

RD Understanding your context, engaging in a diverse community, exploring previously unconnected things, and putting curiosity into action – that makes me think if your focus on curiosity impacts your relationship to external stakeholders. Do customers, external research labs, the start-up community or others, do they see you different than before? What did you observe?

SB Curiosity can clearly help in performance related to customers. Research at INSEAD around curiosity and sales and found that greater curiosity leads to increased sales. There's also research that shows a positive correlation between the curiosity of the CEO and leadership teams, and the long-term success of organizations. From a Novartis perspective, we have seen examples of people being curious leading to better outcomes for our patients. So yes, it clearly makes a difference.

RD Did you see an impact on employer branding?

SB Absolutely. We measure why people want to join our company. We had over 2 million job applications over the last few years, and number one reason people mentioned was the opportunity to learn and develop. So that external visibility around curiosity had a big impact.

RD You are now three years into driving curiosity as a strategic initiative. During this time, you established awareness, conducted interventions, created certain routines. What comes next?

SB Continuing on the journey of curiosity and linking that curiosity through to innovation and experimentation, to skill building and to continuous learning – making sure that people continue to have great opportunities to learn. Separately, my co-authors and I have been working with Hult Ashridge Business School on a diagnostic to measure curiosity for organizations, look out for more coming soon on that!

RD You are not the only organization that talks about the importance of curiosity, but Novartis has managed to create a brand around that value. What makes you different?

Community – is about connecting with a diverse group that provides access to rich resources. Diversity is important here

SB I think we were very deliberate to put culture very high on our agenda. Many organizations don't have that that same level of focus around culture; there may be some values, but it's not necessarily a key priority to shift their culture in such a visible way. We also have been transparent around the journey that we're on and people noticed. I think there's a lot of interest in a large organization going through such a significant culture change, and the lessons learned from it, with what works and what doesn't.

RD I guess your book also helped in this respect.

SB Yes, I would like to think so. It was certainly part of my intent to share through the book the great work that has been done across the teams at Novartis around curiosity, and so others can benefit from what we have learnt.

Simon Brown is Chief Learning Officer at Novartis and co-author of The Curious Advantage.

Roland Deiser is Chairman of the Center for the Future of Organization at the Drucker School of Management and Co-publisher of Developing Leaders Quarterly.

By Stefaan van Hooydonk

Curiosity: A Leadership Trait for Dynamic Times

"Before you are a leader, success is all about growing your-self. When you become a leader, success is all about growing others."—Jack Welch

The shadow that a manager casts on the team is one of the biggest drivers of productivity, engagement, and the feeling of well-being of the team. Those managers who do this well uplift the team. Those who don't stifle it. The key to effective task management and people leadership is curiosity.

Curious organizations are more successful than incurious ones, especially in times of change. Not only are they constantly looking for ways to improve their current operations, but they are also constantly scanning the business horizon for new opportunities. Curious organizations are led by curious leaders.

Curious organizations are constantly scanning the business horizon for new opportunities

Curious leaders are good at operationalizing the present as well as securing the future. They create psychological safety for the team to thrive. Curious leaders represent a high level of cognitive, empathic, and self-reflective curiosity. They are curious about the world around them, the people they work with, and their own internal conscious and unconscious drivers. They go out of their way to engage with their team, also in times of crisis. They stretch their teams to excel in the present and embrace the future. In communicating with others, curious leaders give undivided attention and are mindful in the moment.

Though many leaders see themselves as role models of curiosity and openly say they value inquisitive minds, in fact, many prefer conformity and stifle curiosity within their teams.

However, with the right awareness, intentionality and measurement, leaders can become better at their own curiosity and at the same time create the right curious environment for their teams.

Defining curiosity

Every person is born with a healthy dose of intellectual curiosity. Some people maintain this level through adulthood, many however see their original strength diminish over time. When observing the number of questions children ask, we typically count an average of 75 questions per day. By the time these children become adolescents they ask on average 5-10 questions daily. In some groups it is cool to ask questions, in others not.

By the time these adolescents get into the workforce, many have been conditioned to only ask functional questions: "What do I do to fit in?", "What do I do to stay out of trouble." and "What do I do to please my boss." Some people have escaped this early conditioning and have remained highly curious.

Curiosity is often linked to individuals, yet systems like teams, organizations—even society—can also be curious (or not).

The same happens with systems like start-ups. Early start-ups have a high predisposition to exploration, only to see that this mind-set deteriorates once the company expands, focuses on efficiency, conforms to rigid standards, and finds it harder to learn from mistakes.

In most cultures, curiosity refers to intellectual curiosity. This type of curiosity defines curiosity as the "drive which helps us to make sense of the world around us." It is often linked to surprise and the need to understand things. When reflecting on curiosity, one can also observe two additional aspects of curiosity: our interest in the people around us (empathic curiosity) and our desire to understand our inner selves: our values, our purpose, our deeper (limiting) beliefs (self-reflective curiosity).

Curiosity about the world leads to innovation, curiosity about others leads to empathy and curiosity about our deeper selves leads to resilience, groundedness and a feeling of balance and wellness. Curiosity is often linked to individuals, yet systems like teams, organizations—even society—can also be curious (or not).

Though most leaders say they value inquisitive minds, in fact most stifle curiosity through the conformist cultures they create and through the belief that curiosity jeopardizes efficiency and increases risk

My definition of curiosity, which both encompasses individuals and systems, is the following: "Curiosity is the mindset to challenge the status quo, to explore, discover and learn."

Why curiosity, why now?

Since the beginning of the century and more specifically in the post Covid-19 era, the world of business has been changing dramatically. In times of radical change, leaders realize that milking past successes will not take them very far in the future. As a result, good leaders embrace openness towards an unknown future. Those leaders that balance both exploitation and exploration well keep their organizations competitive. Saying this is easy, doing this is harder. Intentional Curiosity is of paramount importance in times of change.

A 2018 study by the Harvard Business School highlights three insights about importance and implications of workplace curiosity.

1. Curiosity is more important than previously thought. In times of industrial stability, curiosity is limited to continuous improvement as products and services remain relevant for many years. Eastman-Kodak was able to sell its products and services for 100 years given the world of analogue photography did not change much. Once digital photography replaced analogue photography, Eastman-Kodak had lost its exploration mindset. Companies find their environments change constantly and need to be open to respond to changes if they want to remain competitive

2. Companies can change the way they approach curiosity. By making small changes to the design of their organization and the ways they manage employees, leaders can encourage curiosity and improve their companies. When Satya Nadella became CEO at Microsoft in February 2014,

one of the first things he did was to change this ingrained culture of "know-it-all" behaviour. He replaced it with a culture where "learn-it-all" was the norm, where leaders could admit they did not have all the answers and as a result, invite the entire team to collectively come up with the solution.

3. Most leaders stifle curiosity. Though most leaders say they value inquisitive minds, in fact most stifle curiosity through the conformist cultures they create and through the belief that curiosity jeopardizes efficiency and increases risk. On the one hand, executives realize the underlying importance of curiosity in helping to implement their firm's strategy agenda when it comes to product and services innovation, outwitting competition, winning deals, taking calculated risks in the pursuit of novel and creative outcomes, etc. On the other hand, these same executives are rejecting curiosity as something which goes against the grain of operational efficiency of the organization.

Why is workplace curiosity so hard?

Research by the Global Curiosity Institute revealed this say/do disconnect; though 90 percent of leaders believe investing in curiosity to drive innovation is a worthwhile investment, only 50 percent are actively inviting curious behaviour into their own team worried that spending time on innovation distracts the team from being efficient.

In a cross-industry curiosity study funded by the German healthcare and life-sciences giant, Merck, led by curiosity researcher Todd Kashdan, several curiosity barriers associated with leaders were found:

1. Autocratic, top-down leadership behaviour stifles curiosity as curious subordinates are not provided with the opportu-

nity to question or challenge decisions, nor are they invited to explore and share novel options.

2. The prevalence of risk-averse behaviour makes leaders opt for proven and safe ideas, thus restricting creative thinking time.

3. A preference for conformity and fear of standing out from others among managerial peers.

In many organizational cultures, the downside of taking risks is often greater than the upside for managers. Innovation is a lonely business when things go south, and potential failures are limiting career mobility and decrease financial gain.

At the same time, there is a common belief that the positional power of the leader comes with the burden of superior knowledge. Once in power, the leader is supposed to look strong, articulate all questions before the team does, have all the answers. His expert status should not be challenged. In the eyes of the many leaders, not knowing is considered as a sign of weakness. Unbeknownst to many managers however, respect increases every time the manager says 'she does not know' in the team. If at that moment the manager acts with confident humility and invites the team to co-create answers team engagement rises.

Role models

That the daily actions of curious leaders affect team members has been researched by Spencer Harrison, Associate Professor of Organizational Behaviour at INSEAD. Professor Harrison studied the daily logs of teams of scientists working in desert-based Mars simulators. He used linguistic text analysis of team leads and checked how often

Innovation is a lonely business when things go south, and potential failures are limiting career mobility and decrease financial gain

question marks (an indicator of asking questions) were used, as well as exclamation points (a reflection of surprise).

He then correlated this to the logs of the team members in terms of their use of curious language: simply put whether the team members used words like "invent," "create," "discover," "new," "novel," "different," etc. He found a standard deviation in question marks and/or exclamation points the day before also led to a change in standard deviation of the use of curious words of the team members the day after.

Curious leaders invite ideas from their teams and create the right trusting environment, where asking questions, even dissenting ones, is encouraged and celebrated. They are role models and are successful at driving changes given that they are curious individuals themselves. Curious leaders display confident humility: they are not projecting that they know everything. Instead, they are confident to acknowledging openly they don't have all the answers yet are curious to find them together with the team.

Curiosity needs champions. The shadow the manager casts is an important driver for teams. Research by the Global Curiosity Institute has established a linear correlation between the numbers of hours a manager spends on the acquisition of new information and knowledge through reading books or arti-

Curious leaders invite ideas from their teams and create the right trusting environment, where asking questions, even dissenting ones, is encouraged and celebrated

cles, viewing educational videos and taking (e-) classes, listening to podcasts or e-books, and so on. The more the manager consumes new knowledge, the more the team also follows in the curious behavioural footsteps of the leader. As a result, there is an increase in the hours the team spends on learning to mimic those of the leader. Intuitively this makes sense.

When the manager is curious herself, she will—openly or not—make it clear she values new knowledge in the team. The team will recognize that learning and intellectual exploration is important and will follow the manager's example.

The reverse sadly is also true. If a manager does not communicate in words or—more importantly in actions—that learning is important, the team stops to grow and learn too.

In short: good managers uplift the team and stretch it beyond what they thought was feasible. Bad managers, on the other hand, stifle the team and hold it back. Few companies are actively measuring the effectiveness of their leaders with data, even fewer companies are proactively targeting individualized training and coaching for leaders receiving critical scores from their teams.

How leaders can get better at curiosity

Curiosity is a muscle, just like any muscle in the physical body. The more we use it, the bigger and stronger it gets. Stop using it, and it atrophies, becomes weak, and is prone to damage. With the right awareness and with objective measurement, we can all learn to become intentionally curious leaders. The opportunity for leaders is dual. Firstly, leaders can become (even) more productively curious as professionals themselves and secondly, leaders can create a conducive environment in their team and thus invite curiosity to flourish.

In both instances there are three concepts to keep in mind: *Awareness, Intentionality* and *Measurement*.

Awareness is the result of proactive third person reflection, namely observing oneself through the eyes of an outsider. Once one is aware of the status-quo, the leader has the opportunity to change those areas which can need to be strengthened. When this is clear, qualitative and quantitative measurements can be used to baseline and keep track of ongoing progress.

Curiosity is a muscle, just like any muscle in the physical body. The more we use it, the bigger and stronger it gets

To make this actionable: here are some questions:

Awareness: If you are true to yourself, would you say you are an all-round curious individual interested in the world, the people around you, and yourself? When with other people do you find yourself "listening-to-fix" or "listening-to-learn." Are you showing up at work with judgement or with curiosity? Do you ask more 'open' than 'closed' questions? Do the members in your team feel safe to share their ideas and feedback?

Intentionality: Do you have a plan to maintain and strengthen your curiosity about the world, about your relationships with others and about your inner drivers? Are you putting curiosity on the team agenda? Are you identifying barriers to curiosity in the team, creating quick wins and building on their successes? Are you openly inviting the team to co-create a curious environment?

Measurement: Are you asking for reverse feedback from your team and asking them how well you are doing? Are you asking your peers or employees how curious you are showing up in meetings? Are you open to baseline your own curiosity as well as that of the team?

Stefaan van Hooydonk is founder of the Global Curiosity Institute and author of The Workplace Curiosity Manifesto. *This text is adapted from the leadership chapter of his book.*

www.globalcuriosityinstitute.com

Saar Ben-Attar with
Mxolisi Mgojo

Igniting an Ecosystem of Curiosity

Mxolisi Mgojo recently retired from Exxaro Resources as CEO. His career to that position has been led by curiosity, from humble beginnings in the South African countryside, through an engineering degree and then entrepreneurial mining start-up with Eyesizwe Coal and the consultancy that followed before joining Exxaro 16 years ago as a General Manager of one of its operations and then rising through the business. In conversation with DLQ Africa editor, Saar Ben Attar, he shares how his desire to always understand what lies over the horizon and how it might affect his current operations, his curiosity drive, has informed his behaviour and underpinned his success, from tending the family livestock to leading a major South African corporation.

Introduction

As we sit down at Paul's, an elegant coffee shop in the leafy northern suburbs of Johannesburg, Mxolisi casts his mind to when he first became an avid learner, full of curiosity, in his early life. We speak about what sparked curiosity in him, how he grew to become a curious leader and, in heading one of South Africa's leading resources & energy companies, he reached beyond the organization's borders, to ignite an ecosystem of curiosity.

Becoming a curious learner

Raised in the rolling hills of the Eastern Cape Province of South Africa, home to leaders such as Nelson Mandela, Oliver Tambo and others, Mxolisi experienced a rural upbringing, where taking responsibility for the family's stock of sheep and cattle was of the utmost importance. Curiosity was simply not a term used in the household. There were daily challenges to overcome and responsibilities to assume, from a young age. He explains 'Dealing with challenging situations from an early age teaches one to persevere.' However, between the many responsibilities which young Mxolisi was tasked with, curiosity was often within reach. Curiosity was a valuable ally to an inexperienced Mxolisi, as the necessities of daily life required him to seek new solutions. During his 20's, he found himself in what he later called a 'crisis of identity', with a deep sense of responsibility to fulfil his parents' wishes for him becoming a Doctor, while he found himself drawn to and becoming increasingly curious about other professions. He enrolled to study Pre-Med studies in

Curiosity was a valuable ally to an inexperienced Mxolisi, as the necessities of daily life required him to seek new solutions

the US and found himself curious about a range of electives offered during his studies. He was particularly drawn to Computer Studies. These were the 1980's, when personal computers began to appear across the US and colleges were offering Computer Science degrees, an opportunity which Mxolisi took on and quickly shifted from medicine to this growing field. Graduating with a BSc in Computer Science from Northeastern University, his curiosity has already begun to shape his professional life.

In reflecting on those days, Mxolisi acknowledges the roles which challenge and necessity played as he grew to become a curious and avid learner. 'Not seeing another option worked in my favour' he says. 'It pushed me in new directions, and I was curious to find what may lie just beyond the horizon', whether herding livestock on his ancestral land or finding himself in the fast-paced life of a burgeoning computer industry. Returning to South Africa provided him with an opportunity to practice curiosity, this time in leadership.

Curiosity as the Leader's work

Opportunities can truly ground us as leaders. Faced with audacious goals, which our curiosity has drawn us to and recognizing the responsibility thrust upon us, curiosity was about to play a vital role, once again, in Mxolisi's life. In 1994, South Africa

Mxolisi's curiosity was driving him to explore new roles and investment banking seemed a fitting place to practice his curiosity in deal-making

became a young democracy and many of those living in the African diaspora began to return to their homeland and participate in growing a more inclusive economy. The Resources and Energy sectors were to play a critical role in this economic transition, as new consortiums and black-owned business groups began to secure and grow a portfolio of assets in these sectors.

The Eyesizwe group was one, led by Sipho Nkosi. Sipho was on the lookout for young talent who could help lead South Africa's first takeover of a mining group by previously disadvantaged entrepreneurs and his eye caught a young leader, turned investment banker, who recently returned to the country. At the same time, Mxolisi's curiosity was driving him to explore new roles and investment banking seemed a fitting place to practice his curiosity in deal-making, of which more were to follow. What began as an informal chat over coffee turned into an offer and Mxolisi found himself as part of the team that would lead the successful merger of Eyesizwe Coal with Kumba Resources' non-iron ore assets to form Exxaro Resources in 2006. The transaction was hailed as the deal of the year and provided Mxolisi with an opportunity to bring curiosity into growing the merged entity. Exxaro Resources grew from what many analysts saw as an undervalued set of assets to a $1.5 billion market cap industry player, by 2020.

Taking on a number of roles in the newly acquired organization, Mxolisi was posing new questions which ignited curiosity not only in himself but in others, who worked with him. He recalls mentors who introduced him to international commodity markets, for example. His curiosity allowed him to be influenced by them, to remain open. He recalls 'The smarter they were, the more I wanted to learn from them.' This practice of curiosity also extended to colleagues who were assessing new growth opportunities for the group. Recognizing this diverse group of young talent, who shared his ambition for a purpose-driven Exxaro Resources, he often reminded himself of the human-centered approach which they shared, over many and deep conversations. He added 'At the core of our humanity, we all want to self-actualize.'

Curiosity invokes powerful questions

By this stage, leadership curiosity was turning into keen commercial interests taking shape within the group, as it aimed to grow internationally, as well as in South Africa's Waterberg region, a resource-rich yet under-developed region in the north of the country, bordering Botswana. Unlocking the value of this region required seeing the region's potential, beyond the caution which was expressed amongst many groups, from the Board, to business leaders and parastatals (semi-autonomous government agencies), tasked with growing road and rail links.

Such a growth path required a compelling and shared ambition, to which various stakeholders could commit. He recalls posing the question to a rail executive: 'Really, why can't it be done?' and comparing tapping the region's growth potential to an adventure. This helped draw others into a more critical examination of the challenges which lay before them.

Curiosity began to galvanize into a shared sense of adventure, as he won shareholder approval for spending approximately $1.2 billion on this planned operation. The result was the Grootegeluk mine, one of the world's largest coal mining complexes and a new power station being built by the country's electricity utility, in response to the electricity shortages of recent years. Similarly, building a portfolio of new mineral assets and clean energy projects took shape, the latter in partnership with Tata Power (Exxaro Resources later acquired Tata's 50% stake in 2020, reaffirming their commitment to clean energy.)

He recalls posing the question: 'Really, why can't it be done?'

Digitization as a foundation for growth

Mxolisi noticed many new ideas emerging from the people around him. He says 'I began to see new ideas emerging – it galvanized my belief that you invest in people first to create the foundation for people to showcase their curiosity, learning to solve new problems cross-functionally, and being recognized and rewarded for their curiosity.'

In 2017, Mxolisi succeeded Sipho Nkosi as the Group CEO of Exxaro Resources. One could have expected he would follow in his predecessor's path, but his curiosity led him elsewhere, challenging the purpose of the group, right at its core. Within a short while, the Business of Tomorrow was established, where talent from around the group was given an opportunity to explore new trends and imagine the future of the business from new perspectives – from a business focused on the local market to a purpose extending across Africa and the world, from fossil fuels to clean energy and from a profitable core business, challenged by Climate Change, to multiple core businesses, which power a clean world, in minerals and energy.

Mxolisi recognized that curiosity can extend to the edges of the organization, and how he engaged teams across the business would determine whether they feel empowered and have a sense of agency to explore new ways of working and being. I came across Mxolisi's immense impact on the people of Exxaro shortly after we began to work with the group. On an Innovation Day out at an offsite venue, the excitement was palpable. Team after team were showcasing their experimentation and learnings in digital transformation, finding new solutions and pathways to growth, from improved logistics to patented mineral screening processes, which the group licensed to others. While the atmosphere was festive, this was serious fun.

Curiosity at the center of Ecosystem leadership

Reimagining a proud and successful business requires us to venture beyond our borders – organizational borders, industry paradigms and long-held beliefs, which may have sustained the business in the past but possibly no longer. Mxolisi recalls asking his team 'What if we set the bar really high? What could we achieve and with whom?'. This led to igniting new ideas well beyond the organization's borders and building new ecosystems.

An example would be his work at Talent10, an investment holding company, whose mission is to create businesses that have a worldwide, long-term social and economic impact. The Talent10 team recognized that they could build a diverse portfolio, fuelled by the growth in digital technologies and the opportunities opening-up in the media space, in emerging markets. One could have settled for a bar set low, but fuelled by curiosity, asking what may lie just beyond the horizon, brought Mxolisi and team to seek veteran studio executive and producer Simon Swart, CEO of its independent film company Nthibah Pictures, and Los Angeles based US subsidiary, NTB Pictures. Together, they built an ecosystem where creative voices from the US, South Africa, and countries outside the main film hubs,

Mxolisi recognized that curiosity can extend to the edges of the organization, and how he engaged teams across the business would determine whether they feel empowered and have a sense of agency to explore new ways of working and being

could showcase their authentic stories, using a new distribution structure. Drawing on Mxolisi's question some years back, they asked 'Really, why can't it be done?' and then got to work, ignited curiosity in those around them – from independent directors to local talent, for ambitious projects to take shape – profitably and beyond the established film industry.

We see curiosity-driven journeys such as this across many client organizations. Curious leaders bring an innate sense of wonder, an open mindset and new perspectives to some of the world's greatest challenges. We see leadership teams embrace diversity of thought and of practice, and together, anticipate the future in new ways, back-casting to discover more effective pathways to todays' realities and where they can make decisions and position themselves for a future that is, a least in part, already here. The impact which Mxolisi and his partners helped create, is a testament to what is possible when we allow curiosity to lead us, inspiring some of their biggest detractors to pause, reconsider and ultimately participate in building new, highly valued networks. In the process, they change themselves and create the mechanisms, from conversation forums to thought provoking nudges, from digital networks to new ventures and a web of partners where curiosity is practiced, and which all makes this possible at greater scale. They become a driver of value in the digital economy which continues to take shape around us and new opportunity spaces in which we can play, with curiosity at heart. They have not only outperformed their industry peers by nearly 2:1 (measured by Total Shareholder Returns, over a 10-year period) but brought new solutions to some of the world's greatest challenges.

Curious leaders bring an innate sense of wonder, an open mindset and new perspectives to some of the world's greatest challenges.

Mxolisi Mgojo *is co-founder of Investment Holding Company Talent10 and Business Leader of the Year, All Africa Business Leaders Awards (AABLA) in 2022. During his time as an executive at Exxaro Resources, he has helped grow the firm's value to $1.5Billion and shift the group into building a future-fit business portfolio, spanning minerals and energy assets.*

Saar Ben-Attar *is the founder of growth & innovation firm Ascent Growth Partners, with offices in Singapore and South Africa. He is an Executive Fellow at the Center for the Future of Organization at the Peter E. Drucker School of Management, and serves also as an associate editor (Africa) at* Developing Leaders Quarterly.

By Bay Jordan

Human Capital Accounting

How You Can Avoid Bad Business Practice

How often have you heard it? Possibly you have even said it. *"Our people are our greatest asset."* The statement is so common it has become a cliché. Clichés often start life however as a new insight, and just lose value through overuse—so we should not ignore this phrase just because it is platitudinous .

The rationale

It has been said that people constitute 70-80% of the value of a business. Jack Welch, the former CEO of GE famously said *"We know where most of the creativity, the innovation, the stuff that drives productivity lies – in the minds of those closest to the work."* At its most elemental, business is just human activity: people providing things for other people. Ultimately, running a business is about co-ordinating the activities of people, and this demands people skills and leadership. It is therefore only logical to acknowledge that people are assets that comprise the core value of any business.

How can we ever expect to have engaged, enthusiastic employees when, even if we keep telling them they are valued assets, every action subtly reinforces the message that they are actually no more than a cost?

We are therefore entirely justified in claiming that employees are our greatest asset. The problem is we don't account for, manage or treat them as such. If we did, surely we would include them on the balance sheet with all our other assets? And yet we don't. But it's not really our fault. Generally Accepted Accounting Practice (GAAP) insists upon accounting treatment that ultimately treats people exclusively as *costs*. This has serious consequences.

The consequences

In the land where profit is king and employees are one of our biggest expenditures, we will always look to our people to reduce costs. We justify almost any new investment by the number of people we save. Learning and Development (L&D) is often a battleground between HR and Finance—to the detriment of the employee. And when times get tough, it is more likely than not we will consider redundancy as a solution. This is almost a reflex, knee-jerk reaction—despite the fact redundancy payments actually entail *additional* costs—at least initially. And unfortunately, the same mindset prevails in non-profit institutions too.

How can we ever expect to have engaged, enthusiastic employees when, even if we keep telling them they are valued assets, every action subtly reinforces the message that they are actually no more than a cost? And sometimes not so subtly!

The action recently taken by P&O Ferries, the major UK shipping company, highlights an extreme example of this kind of activity. In March this year P&O Ferries dramatically made 800 of their 3000 UK-based employees redundant with *immediate* effect. This decision and the brutal way it was initiated—by a recorded video message—provoked outrage from all corners: employees, unions, politicians and commentators and, the outrage only increased as more was learned.

Notwithstanding his admission that the underhand action was likely illegal and taken to replace those employees with foreign workers whom they wished to pay less than the legal UK minimum wage rate, the CEO, Peter Hebblethwaite, admitted to parliament he would repeat it if he had to. Something he justified on the grounds that the company was not viable without the intended savings.

The leadership gaffe

P&O Ferries' treatment of employees was more than the *"slap in the face"* described by the press. It was also commercially short-sighted, showing a complete disregard for employees' shared history and past contribution, but also their rights, dignity, thoughts and feelings. What is also abundantly clear is that there was no recognition of employees as assets. On the contrary, the whole tactic took no account of their value or the accumulated expertise they offered: things like the teamwork, safety needs, where things are stored, etc. Add in the costs of redundancy, the loss of goodwill—of both customers and employees—and the legal costs which arose from the

P&O Ferries' treatment of employees was more than the "slap in the face" described by the press.

nature and volume of the outrage and it all became a massive PR disaster. As a result, the short-term costs will have been considerably more than expected while the longer-term costs are also likely to be greater, even ignoring the experience lost which would be needed to restore effective operations. Thus, it is dubious whether they achieved any of the benefits hoped for and perhaps calls into question whether they have only increased the likelihood of the very consequences they were taken to avoid.

Yet the P&O Ferries case is perhaps only an extreme example of the need for—and failure of—managers to also be leaders. Open a newspaper or listen to a news report on almost any day and you will find other examples. Just think of the post-pandemic chaos currently being experienced by airlines and airports. Or the industrial action being taken by railway workers in the UK and being threatened by teachers, NHS workers, doctors and police; the latter two who are not even allowed to strike.

THE REAL PROBLEM

Many headlines described the P&O Ferries debacle as an example of the ugly side of capitalism. Such claims merely politicize the issue and add no real substance to a subject that needs to be properly addressed and promptly rectified. However culpable P&O Ferries are for their management decisions, they did nothing more than shine a light on an extreme case of poor business leadership and practice.

The situation arose from a "profits before people" corporate philosophy. Our current state of affairs shows the problem runs deeper. This kind of decision-making is simply the inevitable consequence of executives failing to recognize the value of people, and accounting for, managing and treating employees exclusively as a cost.

Here Jack Welch once again provided a useful insight saying, *"If the rate of change on the outside exceeds the rate of change on the inside, the end is near."* It certainly seems that the rate of change is greater than we can handle at present. So, it definitely appears to be time to do things differently.

Enlightened executives *do* speak of people as being their greatest asset. Yet they also persist in accounting for employees entirely as a cost. Businesses thus continue to be able to make their employees redundant without any concept of the value they are discarding. In the process they all make the same mistakes as P&O Ferries and:

Just think of the post-pandemic chaos currently being experienced by airlines and airports

- Destroy value;
- Fail to take advantage of the very resources that could best help them solve the problems they are trying to address;
- Jeopardize longer term performance and results for 'apparent' (but possibly dubious) short term benefits;
- Fail to properly meet what has traditionally (but perhaps erroneously) been cited as their primary fiduciary responsibility: to safeguard shareholders' investments.

Let's take a closer look at these points.

Destroy value

Regardless of the fact that they are not reflected as assets on the Balance Sheet people *are* corporate assets. Without them you cannot fulfil your corporate objectives or achieve any of the things you set out to achieve. Remember the old nursery rhyme about the kingdom that was lost for the want of a horseshoe nail? The same applies to any corporation: every employee plays a part in fulfilling a role that enables delivery of the corporate purpose. Dispensing with people with no regard for their value detracts from the overall value of the corporation. The intellectual capability, and years of knowledge of how everything fits, walks out of the door with them. It's like losing part of a set; the value of the set is reduced when any part is damaged.

Regardless of the fact that they are not reflected as assets on the Balance Sheet people are corporate assets. Without them you cannot fulfil your corporate objectives or achieve any of the things you set out to achieve

Failure to take advantage of resources

It was Ken Blanchard that said, *"All of us are smarter than any of us."* Unfortunately, this is a lesson that many executives have failed to learn and so get caught up in their own hubris. It certainly seems to be what happened at P&O Ferries. I am convinced they could have achieved annual savings of considerably more than anything they hoped to achieve, and certainly more than they now look like achieving, if they had only approached their people honestly and discussed the situation with them more openly. Instead, their approach—evidenced by Hebblethwaite's statement that he would "do the same again"—lends itself to a belief in their executive's exclusive intelligence and ability: something little different from the ancient "divine right of kings." Making people redundant at any time, but particularly in a recession, is likely to handicap your position and slow your progress when things improve.

Jeopardize the longer-term for the short-term

Reducing employment costs is pretty much a knee-jerk reaction of executive management to poor results or changing trading conditions. This ought to be fairly easily identified when corporations are ready to contemplate incurring "short-term", one-off costs in order to save future costs. It is clearly evident in the P&O Ferries example with the company being prepared to pay significant redundancy costs in order to reduce their ongoing salary charge, as well as the likely "fallout" costs of their decision to do things the way they chose. This compounds the loss of value and makes these costs more difficult to recover and likely to take longer—because you no longer have the people who would enable you to do so. P&O Ferries pursued a route that will make it very difficult to re-establish the viability of their business if their action fails to provide the "Hail Mary" solution that its executives opted for.

Failure to meet fiduciary responsibilities

If P&O Ferries intended to safeguard their shareholders' best interests they have certainly achieved the opposite. But that is the least of it. There is increasing recognition of the need for business to move beyond focusing on shareholders and to meet all stakeholders' needs. This demands wider recognition of business as part of an ecosystem; operating as part of the wider community and thus recognizing the community as one of its stakeholders. (Surely what Corporate Social Responsibility (CSR) is all about?) It would seem P&O Ferries failed to meet *any* stakeholder's interests, least of all those of the community. Their disregard for the laws is prima facie evidence of that. They may be unique in that, but not in the general effect of their efforts, which is to transfer living costs from the company to the community. (People who aren't earning in the UK are entitled to "benefits" which are paid for by the taxpayer.) This is hardly being a "good corporate citizen."

The whole P&O Ferries saga was unquestionably an unethical fiasco that raises some very serious questions about the executives running the company. But it runs deeper than that. The way that this has been allowed to happen and its portrayal as "the ugly side of capitalism" highlights the major weakness in our accounting systems and practices. It is imperative that we find a way to start valuing our people as assets and take greater cognizance of their value and contribution to our corporations and businesses.

"All of us are smarter than any of us."

The Solution

If the problem is the failure to recognize people as assets, the solution is obvious: reverse this and recognize people as assets. Of course, that is easier said than done. This is because valuing people in a consistent way is a challenge. My three-step Every Individual Matters Model is the basis for addressing that challenge and as a means to avoid P&O Ferries type problems.

The first step is pivotal and is the valuation: incorporating a formula for determining an initial value for each and every employee, which is aggregated and held as "Human Assets" in a notional balance sheet account. Thereafter the challenge lies in accounting for changes in value over time. These are determined by identifying key criteria of any specific role and adjusting the value proportionately for any notable shifts in accordance with pre-determined rules. This would include such circumstances as changes in role, hours, responsibility etc. but, most inventively, by increasing value by capitalizing a fixed portion of any training and development program the employee undertakes. This creates a process where training costs are balanced by a notional increase in asset value, in the same way that other assets are enhanced with additional investment, and so should encourage finance directors to direct money towards training rather than away from it.

Although GAAP would not currently permit this to be incorporated in published accounts there is nothing to prevent us doing all this in the internal management accounts.

This demands wider recognition of business as part of an ecosystem; operating as part of the wider community and thus recognizing the community as one of its stakeholders.

Perhaps the most controversial aspect to this approach is that there is a fixed factor used in the formula for the initial valuation. This facilitates the consistency, universality and ultimate equitability of the valuation process, but favours the lower paid employees. This is needed to help close the ever-widening income disparity that underlies so many of the industrial and societal problems we face. This rationale will become clearer from the next two steps, but it is essential to create the shift in the workplace that will otherwise remain elusive and leave us with traditional worker versus management conflict and the kinds of problems we have been reviewing.

Step Two entails the creation of a Human Capital Account. This is necessary to balance the Human Asset Account and keep the balance sheet in balance. However, by treating this as part of Owners' Equity you create the capability to give each and every employee a 'virtual' ownership stake in the business equal to their asset value. This creates all the benefits of employee ownership without any of the drawbacks of traditional employee ownership schemes or share stocks, and is a much more effective means of engaging employees and encouraging a culture where everyone thinks like an owner of the business. It creates a partnership between the individual and the corporation to optimize the value of the individual, for the ultimate benefit of both.

Protest at P&O head office at the sacking of 800 workers. Shutterstock / Philip Robinson

Step Three takes the virtual ownership to the next level. By rewarding employees through a "labour dividend" paid on the same basis and at the same rate as the traditional share dividend. This recognizes employees' 'life' investment and allows them to share in the risks and rewards of the business in the same way as capital investors, but without diluting the latter's stakes. Applicable even if there are no shareholders, it is cost neutral if it replaces an existing bonus pool and most incentive-based remuneration. It also offers a considerably fairer and more equitable basis of reward while recognizing the integrity of the business as a single entity.

Increasing value by capitalizing a fixed portion of any training and development program the employee undertakes, and so should encourage finance directors to direct money towards training rather than away from it.

The model's main attraction is its simplicity, and while no doubt requiring some tailoring when put into practice in different businesses, I believe it can square the circle around creating a mindset where employees are truly viewed as assets. Once we start to see how valuable our people are, on the balance sheet as well as on the ground, attitudes will change around how we handle them—in the same way as we treat other expensive assets. We will not 'slash and burn' them at the first sign of trouble, but instead will naturally lean towards investing in their development and caring for them better. This will lead to those 'assets' then feeling more valued themselves, and just that fact, unlike with a piece of expensive machinery, will elicit greater productivity and engagement.

Bay Jordan describes himself as a different sort of accountant. After qualifying as a Chartered Accountant in Zimbabwe and South Africa he spent 8 years in public practice before moving into financial management and consultancy, working in blue chip organizations in South Africa, North America and the UK. Recently relocated to Scotland, he is a published author and motivational speaker and enabler.

By Henrik Cronqvist and Désirée-Jessica Pély

The Social CEO: Just Human After All

As chief executive officers (CEOs) undertake the role of top ambassadors of their firms, oftentimes becoming well-known public figures, their reputations inevitably become linked to the success of their companies. These top leaders work hard to maintain a reputable image to cultivate the firm's potential to thrive. Part of that effort includes assuming mostly purely professional personas, where they have mastered the art of leaving their social and human dimensions at home—so only the business leader arrives at work, ready to steer the ship towards profit maximization.

Societal regard largely dictates the tendency towards this division between the professional and social self. We collectively imagine that these managers at the pinnacles of their careers invariably embody business-minded mavens who can connect the dots, from finance to marketing to global expansion and all the connected areas of business, without letting personal influences interfere in corporate decisions. Under this societal view, top leaders face pressure to maintain ethical standards and managerial leadership dedicated to profit and forming positive consumer opinion; they are only able to resume their social selves once away from the mental frameworks and social constructs of the business.

Yet, though we may have become accustomed to this rather two-dimensional view of the CEO, these leaders are not exempt from a human being's natural tendency to carry the layers of their personality, ideologies, and social identities into most aspects of their lives, unavoidably seeping into the realm of their professional existence. CEOs, like humans more generally, are a product of their environment, beginning from birth and continuing with the various experiences throughout life. The compilation of these experiences determines not only the individual's human and social aspects but also the policy direction of their firm. In this manner, the firm becomes a reflection of the social CEO, with traits that are inescapable even unto themselves.

Life experiences may stem from occurrences that originate externally, independent of one's own choices, as well as from personal choices and individual traits. In either case, the effects of lived events shape leadership styles in subtle yet impactful ways.

External events

External forces influence chief executives' world views, which in turn influence the policies that they implement. A parent does not choose whether to have a son or a daughter, for instance. Yet, CEOs who have daughters lead with more social responsibility than those without daughters, as shown in a 2017 study [www.ideasforleaders.com/ideas/how-a-daughter-might-shape-the-ceo], conducted by one of the authors of this article, Cronqvist, along with colleague Frank

CEOs who have daughters lead with more social responsibility than those without daughters

Yu. Specifically, a CEO with a daughter engages the firm in more corporate social responsibility (CSR) endeavours, paying more attention to areas such as employee relations and social and environmental well-being as encouraged by their parenting experience.

Early life circumstances similarly shape individuals in unexpected ways. 'Depression baby' CEOs, or those who grew up during the Great Depression and later in life became leaders of firms, carry the effects of the early circumstantial impacts into their decision-making. These CEOs show less willingness to take financial risk and less likelihood to participate in the stock market, as revealed in a 2011 study by Ulrike Malmendier and Stefan Nagel. By the same token, however, individuals who have experienced high stock market returns show less hesitation towards financial risks, participate more readily in the stock market, and allocate a higher proportion of their liquid asset portfolio to risky assets.

Beyond the Great Depression, results of the study help explain reactions to stretches of either flourishing or discouraging stock market periods. Low stock market participation of young households in the early 1980s, for instance, resulted from disappointing returns in the 1970s, and the high participation of young investors in the late 1990s reflected the boom years of that decade. But their findings indicate that, though more recent financial return experiences have a stronger influence, experiences early in life still carry a significant effect, even several decades later. An early personal economic shock, such as that induced by the Great Depression, affects leaders' attitudes towards risk well into their later years.

Relatedly, the socioeconomic status during one's upbringing, such as growing up in a working-class household, prompts certain policy tendencies that affect company culture. In a 2019 analysis on the subject, Cronqvist, Irena Hutton, and Danling Jiang found that chief executives who come from a low socioeconomic background lead firms with more labour issues than those who were raised in more affluent homes. CEOs who were exposed to low levels of employee welfare as children are less likely to promote employee-friendly labour policies in the firms that they manage. Firms run by CEOs raised in low socioeconomic class undergo more employment and labour litigation, more workplace health and safety violations, and a lower level of overall employee satisfaction with multiple dimensions of firm policies.

Person-specific events

Events that occur due to personal decisions may also create character-molding forces that impact firm governance. When an individual makes the personal decision to join the military, for instance, he or she becomes exposed to militaristic

Findings indicate that, though more recent financial return experiences have a stronger influence, experiences early in life still carry a significant effect, even several decades later

discipline, viewpoints, and, potentially, wartime and battle. If such a person moves on to become a CEO of a company, they are likely to lead with more inclination towards conservative investment and financial policies, as scholars Efraim Benmelech and Carola Frydman found in their 2015 study. Firms run by CEOs who have served in the military tend to invest less, have lower expenditures on research and development, and pursue slightly lower leverage ratios than their non-military counterparts. Moreover, the management style of CEOs with a military background appears to be more resilient to crisis and fraud, as military training likely instills a strong sense of ethics. Military CEOs are significantly less likely to be involved in corporate fraudulent activity and tend to perform better during times of industry distress.

However, military service brings into question the factor of choice, or the dynamic between externally or internally influenced events. Military experience becomes exogenous and not optional in times of a military draft. Someone drafted into the military would likely experience military life and the hardships of battle, but not from their own volition. If this individual moves on to become a chief executive of a company, he may likely employ a related leadership style with similar outcomes as mentioned above. But the traits that led to these outcomes were ingrained outside of the manager's power to become a different individual, which may have led to differing policy choices. Both drafted and non-drafted military CEOs may end up with the same leadership style, but not by choice, expounding the reality that life shapes the leaders and not necessarily the other way around.

Even an internal identity trait, such as one's name, molds leaders and their governance approaches. A recent **study** by Yungu Kang, David Zhu, and Yan Anthea Zhang shows that an

The management style of CEOs with a military background appears to be more resilient to crisis and fraud, as military training likely instills a strong sense of ethics.

unconventional name, as an internalized trait that one carries throughout life, can point to an unconventional leader, or one that leads a firm with strategic distinctiveness. An individual with an uncommon name tends to develop a conception of being different from peers, and CEOs under this scenario tend to see themselves as different from other CEOs in their industry. These leaders have surpassed potential challenges associated with being different and usually develop a high sense of confidence to tackle potential adversities associated with distinctive strategies.

As CEOs are usually confident individuals, those with uncommon names tend to view themselves as capable of achieving successful outcomes through strategies that differ from those of their peers. These CEOs pursue strategies that deviate from industry norms especially when they carry more confidence and hold more power, as well as when they operate in an environment with more growth opportunities. Elon Musk, for example, is known for leading his ventures with irregular strategies and with openness to strategic changes and innovation. He leads typically unconventional firms based on unconventional ideas.

A CEO's divorce serves as another scenario that carries ripples into corporate policy making. When a couple undergoes a personal choice like divorce, CEOs in this situation adjust leadership decisions based on their concern for personal wealth. In 2019, University of Melbourne researcher Jordan Neyland found that CEOs going through a divorce lose incentive to take on corporate risk. As divorcing top managers experience a significant wealth reduction during divorce settlements, such as in cash or real estate, their portfolios become less diversified and more concentrated on the firm's stock holdings, decreasing their motivation to explore riskier corporate moves.

Ironically, while divorce signifies a usually detrimental life experience and marriage generally a happy one, both life events lead to similar impact on the CEO's approach to risk. Earlier research by Nikolai Roussanov and Pavel Savor reveals that a married CEO will more frequently refrain from risk-prone activities as compared to single CEOs. The difference in risk aversion indicates that marital status sways the leader's

Elon Musk, for example, is known for leading his ventures with irregular strategies and with openness to strategic changes and innovation. He leads typically unconventional firms based on unconventional ideas.

risk preferences. A married CEO will generally engage less readily in activities like capital expenditures, R&D, advertising, and acquisitions. Their single counterparts, meanwhile, prove more open to risk, but also lead firms that exhibit higher stock return volatility.

Behavioural consistency

Insights on the self and associations to leadership styles extend to the notion of behavioural consistency. A constancy of behaviour, or the tendency of individuals to behave consistently across situations, creates patterns of behaviour in managers that encompass the policy direction of their firms. In a 2012 study, Cronqvist and colleagues Anil Makhija and Scott Yonker assessed top managers' level of personal debt tolerance by analyzing information on CEOs' primary homes and mortgages, since mortgage debt tends to be the most important source of debt. Compared to their use of corporate leverage during their tenures, they found that CEOs with lower debt

Top executives with a high ownership rate of luxury goods, including expensive cars, boats, and houses, usually lead a loose corporate environment at their firms

tolerance manage firms that exhibit more conservative corporate capital structures, suggesting that leaders of firms imprint their personal preferences on the capital structures of the companies that they manage.

Political ideology also carries over to corporate financial views. A study in the Journal of Financial and Quantitative Analysis reveals that personal political preferences significantly determine corporate policies. In the US, Republican CEOs, who usually hold conservative personal views, pursue more conservative financial policies than do Democrats. On average, Republican managers have lower levels of corporate debt, lower capital and R&D expenditures, and less propensity to engage in risky investments. They tend to lead firms with lower volatility of stock returns in correlation with a safer capital structure and investment policies.

Other off-the-job behaviours also extend with consistency into the workplace. Scholars in one analysis showed that executives with low frugality and with past legal infractions, such as driving under the influence, drug-related charges, domestic violence, reckless behaviour, disturbing the peace, and traffic violations, have a higher probability of financial reporting risks during their leadership role. In fact, CEOs and CFOs with a legal record are more likely to commit fraud, as reflected in such an executive being named for fraudulent corporate reporting in an Accounting and Auditing Enforcement Release by the Securities and Exchange Commission.

Meanwhile, top executives with a high ownership rate of luxury goods, including expensive cars, boats, and houses, usually lead a loose corporate environment at their firms. The approach generates an increased probability of other insiders engaging in fraud and unintentional material reporting errors, especially as impacts become more pronounced over the non-frugal CEO's tenure. This governance style usually produces cultural changes that may include the appointment of an unfrugal CFO, an increase in executives' equity-based incentives to misreport, and an environment of less board monitoring intensity, all of which may increase fraud risk.

But whether behaviours stem from external or personal events, and whether they reflect behavioural consistency or 'of the moment' situations such as divorce, life experiences allow for varying CEO leadership styles. The various scenarios of imprinted CEO personality on firm policies demonstrate that, even in business, human nature is inescapable. And yet this inescapability colours the corporate world. If you remove CEO human and social layers, corporate leadership would likely result in mostly homogenous policies and outcomes, with firms and their leaders looking closer to carbon copies of one another.

If one's experiences outside of the workplace would not influence the professional realm, assertive decisions—including mistakes—would solely be based on numbers and market signals. Global corporate wheels would turn under almost robotic machinery without obvious connections to the cultures

Even in business, human nature is inescapable

and societies that they affect. Instead, the decisions of top-level managers reflect personal, social, human influences that pave a firm's own path and 'character'. Successes and failures of CEOs and firms build stories, teach lessons, and set examples for future leaders. The machinery of business remains intrinsically intertwined with the nuances and experiences of society because its leaders remain social humans after all.

Full references and further reading for this article is available - please contact editor@dl-q.com citing this article with references.

Henrik Cronqvist is Dean and Professor of Finance of the George L. Argyros School of Business and Finance at Chapman University in Orange, California, a position he began on 1 August 2022. He previously served as a professor of finance at the University of Miami School of Business. Cronqvist's research focuses on behavioural, social, and corporate finance with a focus on the behaviour of corporate executives and investors.

Désirée-Jessica Pély is the CEO and Founder of loyee.io. She holds a PhD in Financial and Behavioral Economics from Ludwig-Maximilians Universität München, Miami, and Yale. She has taught 2,500 business, economics, and maths students in finance, risk management, and venture capital.

By Wendy Shepherd

The Trouble With Executive Development

There are very few industries that could charge their clients six or in some cases seven figure sums without any guarantee of the outcomes of their investment. That is often the case with Leadership Development, and there is a very good reason why this happens.

Leadership is a complex activity and leadership perfor-

mance is subject to multiple factors, many of which are beyond the control of any one leader. Furthermore, leadership cannot be taught, it can only be learnt. Yes, there are models and frameworks that can help leaders reflect on their experiences. We can also help broaden perspectives about the organizations within which our clients work and the context within which their organizations operate. But there is no one model of leadership that will work in all contexts. The individual leader needs to decide how to behave within any specific context and learn from both their successes and failures.

If we cannot guarantee the outputs of development, how do we maintain our reputation as an industry and allow our clients to differentiate between suppliers?

I believe that we need to commit to quality in the process

There is no one model of leadership that will work in all contexts

of leadership development rather than collude in the illusion of certainty of outcomes, and that the process of leadership development needs to have impact at its core.

As an industry we need to discuss what does not work within specific contexts, as well as sharing success stories. Having reviewed 116 published case studies of leadership development, less than a quarter referred to any unanticipated or negative outcomes from the development. If we are to continue to learn and innovate, we need to do what we ask our participants to do—learn from both our successes and our failures. That way we can develop a better understanding of the merits and drawbacks of different methods and modes of delivery within specific contexts.

When discussing development objectives, it is common to think in terms of knowledge, skills and behaviours that need to be developed. However, when putting impact at the centre of the development process it is also important to consider how these will generate value in practice.

In this article I describe five case study instances based upon insights from the research into Executive Development I have been conducting over the last 10 years, that highlight where program outcomes can be derailed. The more such awareness we share around these situations the better foundations for successful programs we can implement.

Before we explore these case studies it is worth spotlighting the five impact drivers that link leadership development with changes in the workplace. These drivers are generative mechanisms that explain how impact occurs from leadership development:

- **New conversations and ways of communicating:** These are developed through the application of theory, the socialization of participants, the development of new language, and mimicry. These types of changes in conversation and communication generate future knowledge sharing, learning, coordination and leadership within the organizational context. Many participants go on to share what they have learnt within the development setting with their teams, or initiate their own conversations about the topics discussed.

- **Changes in Sensemaking:** Developed through active reflection, witnessing a breadth of perspectives and the application of theory. Changes in sensemaking generate problem setting and solving, initiate new or amended actions, and changes in tolerance, empathy and commitment within the organizational context.

- **Relationships and Networks:** Developed through the socialization of participants and the socialization of senior sponsors, the development of interpersonal skills and through the application of theory. Relationships are not just interpersonal, they can also be between func-

If we are to continue to learn and innovate, we need to do what we ask our participants to do—learn from both our successes and our failures

tions, units or geographies. Changes in relationships and networks generate access to resources, and create a sense of community, trust and visibility. They also generate beneficial behaviours associated with collaboration, learning, efficiencies and innovation.

- **Alignment of behaviours and priorities:** Developed through presentations, direction, and the leadership of program sponsors (and participants), and the application of common frameworks, observation and mimicry. The alignment of behaviours and priorities has implications for the corporate culture and brand, potentially generating synergies and alliances for change.

- **Engagement**: Generated as a consequence of being labelled as talent, invested in, being inspired by tutors, other participants or program sponsors, and recognizing what is required within specific contexts. Or alternatively being reduced amongst non-participants as a consequence of not being invested in and therefore unintentionally labelled as 'non-talent'. Changes in the engagement of participants and non-participants generate changes in discretionary effort and allegiance to the organization, specific leaders or communities. There is also a multiplying effect through changes in levels of engagement amongst the participants' direct reports as a consequence of improvements in the participants' leadership.

Case A: A reduction in Engagement

A successful family-owned business had a strong culture that did not conform to the business school model of distributed leadership. The chief executive was well connected within industry and government, and made all of the key decisions about which markets were to be entered. He was not up for changing this approach which had proved successful. The development intervention encouraged the participants to explore new markets which they then presented back to the leadership team, who promptly dismissed their ideas. This generated frustration and resentment amongst the participants, many of whom went on to leave the organization. The intention of the investment was to develop leaders that could thrive and succeed within its unique and successful context. Had the models and tools been used to focus on change and improvements within the participants span of control the program may have been more successful.

Although the impact drivers account for many of the organizational changes attributable to the development, they do not automatically generate changes that will be viewed as positive by the sponsoring organization.

Experience has shown that early consultation with clients using the framework of impact drivers, provides a focus for the application of learning that can help generate a positive impact from the delivery. For example, if a client is wishing to increase conversations about Diversity and Inclusion, the models and frameworks of leadership can be used as a lens to explore the leader's role in driving the D&I agenda. Note that this does not necessarily mean that D&I appears as a taught input. Nor does it mean that the participants are encouraged to set the D&I agenda. Rather that they are encouraged to share and explore their understanding of what it means within their organization, and their personal role in delivering against the existing agenda, in the process, sharing ideas and hearing from others who may have faced and overcome similar challenges.

So far, I have suggested how the provider can help design in and manage impact, however, the client also has a critical role to play.

Firstly, they need to be clear about what they wish to achieve and be willing to address any organizational barriers to success. As we know, change is a political process, therefore when used as a tool for organizational change, leadership development is too.Secondly, the client needs to decide which organizational level capabilities they are wishing to develop amongst the leadership team:

Case B: Political Barriers to change

A Chief Executive wished to change his organization's culture from 'command and control' to 'inclusive leadership' in order to navigate a rapidly changing market. To support the change, he invested in leadership development. Although the change was driven from the top, it was not supported by all of his direct reports, some of whom actively undermined the development. Ultimately, it was the Chief Executive's responsibility to align his team in order for the development to be successful. The challenges to the development were identified by a Programe Director who worked very closely with the Chief Executive to address the complexity of change within this context. They learnt what was working and what wasn't working as the development progressed, making changes both within the organization and to the development design in response to the unfolding challenges.

As providers, we can easily misunderstand what our clients mean when they make statements such as they would like their leaders to be more innovative, collaborative or inclusive

Operational Capabilities: In Case A above, the organization was wishing to develop its leaders to operate within the existing mode of operating. The leaders were not required to drive strategic change but to deliver operational performance through incremental changes. For many leaders, this is the reality of their roles, particularly in highly proceduralized, cost sensitive industries such as logistics, retail and manufacturing.

Change Capabilities: In the second example, Case B, the Chief Executive was wishing to develop leaders who were capable of reading and reacting to rapidly changing markets. The leaders were being asked to step up and take responsibility for initiating substantial changes to the way that they served their markets, as well as identifying new markets. Once identified the leaders were required to lead the systemic changes required to deliver upon the new opportunities.

As providers, we can easily misunderstand what our clients mean when they make statements such as they would like their leaders to be more innovative, collaborative or inclusive. Such requirements can be considerably different depending on the context and purpose of leadership within different organizations. Furthermore, there may be differences in the context and therefore the requirement of leaders within the same organization, either across geographies, functions, or business units.

Case C: Different Contexts Different Needs

A head of Learning and Development within the airport retail sector requested a development intervention to increase innovation amongst the leadership population. The sector was losing revenue as a consequence of changes in legislation affecting the tax status of specific products and changes to the rules relating to passenger transportation of liquids. Further probing revealed that the target participants had no control over the products that they stocked or how they served their customers. Innovation in this context was limited to the way they marketed products within the retail space. An input focusing on strategic innovation would have been of little value to the participants and potentially created frustration about the challenges they face yet had no control over.

Finally, the client needs to be clear about the target audience and how to mix participants into cohorts that create value. Often decisions are made about cohort structure without significant thought about the long-term benefits of the relationships developed.

Creating cohorts of leaders from different levels of seniority can create vertical alignment that helps to increase feedback and feedforward of strategic information and distributed leadership. Cohorts that consist of leaders across the organization can help to break down silos and encourage collaboration and coordination. Ad hoc cohorts of leaders randomly selected from the organization may increase informal relationships and networks.

The make-up of cohorts not only affects the development of social capital, but it can also have an impact on how the participants behave and what they are willing to share within the development setting. We often speak about taking the participants away from the work context to reflect, but actually the relationships and organizational culture is present within the development setting, carried-in by the participants themselves.

Within the industry we have many examples similar to the ones I have provided here. The sharing of both our successes and failures within specific contexts can result in innovation and learning within our sector.

Furthermore, we can provide advice to our clients that goes beyond the most popular methods of development or the latest research. As an industry we are often asked to design interventions in accordance with popular thinking, for example '70/20/10'. Methods may be popular but they are rarely universally suited to all contexts and levels of experience. Similarly, as providers, we commonly provide examples of what has worked for other clients, implying that if it worked for them it will work for you, which might not be the case.

Case D: Frustrated Opportunities

A multinational client within the insurance sector commissioned a global leadership program for aspiring leaders. The intention was to increase collaboration and knowledge sharing across geographies, with the aim of generating both innovation and growth. The organization was structured into regions, each of which had autonomy over the products that they provided and the way that they served their markets. The participants were formed into cross-regional teams who explored opportunities for collaboration and growth. The participants gained great insight into each other's markets and were inspired to return to their regions with ideas that required continued collaboration across regions. The regional leaders refused to act upon the ideas of the participants which were inconsistent with the individual regional strategies and targets. The development resulted in a tension between the developing leaders and their line managers, who they considered to be short-sighted. The intervention may have been more successful if the regional heads had been involved in the development, or alternatively the participants had attended the development in regional rather than global groups.

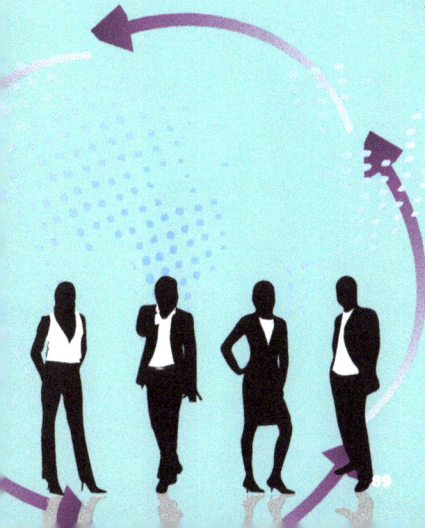

Case E: Culture in the classroom

A large multi-national organization sponsored a development intervention to drive change through the leadership population in terms of their leadership style. The leaders were typically task-focused and competitive. The development design required the participants to share insights and reflect on their experiences. Some cohorts were found to be more open to the development than others. It soon became apparent that the participants were more engaged and willing to share their experiences when they were with people that they already knew and trusted. Furthermore, the behaviour of the participants within the development setting reflected differences in both the national and functional culture of the organization.

If we are to continue to learn and innovate, we need to do what we ask our participants to do—learn from both our successes and our failures

My research has revealed that there is knowledge within our industry that can result in the development of design propositions, which can then be tested and modified through more open debate and sharing of what works, for whom and in which contexts. We may not be able to guarantee the outcomes from our interventions, but we can become impact experts, earning our fees by providing the support and guidance that both our participants and their sponsoring organizations require.

Wendy Shepherd is the Director of Individual and Organisational Impact at Cranfield Executive Development. She has an MBA and Executive Doctorate from Cranfield where her research interest was The Organisational Impact of Executive Development. In 2021 she won the AMBA and BGA doctoral research prize for the impact of her research.

By Katleen De Stobbeleir

Collective Leadership

You can't predict what the future will bring but you can prepare for the challenges ahead. The past two years have made that evident, as organizations in early 2020 found themselves having to pivot and explore new ways of working with almost no warning.

Preparing for the challenges ahead is a task leaders need to ensure gets done despite the continual noises and pressures of daily activity. This leadership should not just come from the top, but leadership that helps to connect the dots throughout an entire organization; leadership that confidently embraces the complexities of today's reality and converts uncertainty and disruption into opportunities for personal and organizational growth.

As we exist in an ever more complex and intricately connected world of increasing uncertainty, leadership in organizations must be prepared to respond appropriately and effectively. Organizations must develop new strategies and forms of leadership to move from hierarchical leadership structures to a more vertical, cooperative leadership approach.

This leadership should not just come from the top, but leadership that helps to connect the dots throughout an entire organization

This is where the concept of 'collective leadership' can be beneficial. So, how can collective leadership help you and your organization build the leadership capabilities today that you will need in the future, and how can this leadership approach be effectively broached within organizations?

Although leadership development starts with a focus on the individual, leadership development should ultimately transform the entire organization, enabling them to operate within a collective leadership approach.

Collective leadership is not the role of any one leader, but the interaction of team members to lead the team by sharing leadership responsibilities. It is not the characteristic of an individual person, but the collaboration of an entire team, group, or organization. As a social process, it is aimed at accomplishing collective rather than individual goals and requires collaborative, coordinated action. True collective leadership occurs when several capable people with complementary strengths and competencies, focused on a compelling purpose and vision, work together to provide direction within a company to contribute to their success.

If you think of an organization like a tower, the stronger, more experienced individuals within a team should be placed at the bottom, to provide a strong based for the structure. This gives a solid foundation for serving the rest of the organiza-

tion. However, the opposite usually occurs, with the stronger members solely placing themselves at the top of the organization which suppresses and exploits the newer, less experienced members.

Impactful leadership development journeys should enhance the mindset as well as the skillsets and toolsets your leaders employ to truly become their best selves. After all, organizations can only truly flourish when individuals within the company grow. However, it is then about cultivating a collective culture within the organization where individual growth and organizational growth go hand-in-hand.

At Vlerick Business School, we noticed that many leadership development programs focus solely on individual leadership skills, imparting knowledge onto students and clients about how to become a better leader—how to improve their interaction style, how to give good feedback, and all the basics needed to become a better individual leader.

However, through our work with organizations, it is apparent that strengthening individuals alone is not enough. Leadership development programs often fail when you train an individual and then send them back to their organization, where they revert to old behaviour patterns and dynamics, which may not have been very effective or adaptable for our ever-changing world.

Developing the system and culture

Organizations need to not just develop individuals as leaders, but also develop a collective group of leaders and have them think about how they can support each other, adapt their organization's culture when necessary, and what collective actions they can take to create a collaborative work culture.

Organizations need to not just develop individuals as leaders, but also develop a collective group of leaders and have them think about how they can support each other

However, there is something influential within a workplace culture that means, whenever we return to that organizational environment or system, it can be hard to practically apply what we have learnt on a leadership development program. This is why we need to pay explicit attention to developing the system and the culture within the organization, not just individuals.

This is where collective leadership can be employed as a way to teach skills as a collective, and teach more skills about how to change culture and get the best out of other managers, while collaborating with other departments. This starts with making values and culture explicit within your organization, understanding them in depth. For example, we run a leadership simulation where participants have to develop a new strategy for a fictional company which is facing difficulties. They start from scratch and decide how to build a project in this new company.

What we typically find is that participants end-up recreating the culture of the company they are already working for, despite having the opportunity to start a project from scratch. We then work with them to identify the strengths of that culture, but also the challenges. Imagine a company that is very good at processes; they might not pay attention to employee emotions or how people are feeling, because they are strongly attached to process. We then have participants reflect on how to bring more emotions to the organization while staying true to the DNA of the culture.

When we work with students or clients, it is about helping them create a roadmap for change, and help them understand that they will go back to their own environment and systemic influences. Just as we help build a roadmap for change, we also give them a roadmap for how to change workplace culture.

Influence and gradual deviation not instant impact

After learning about collective leadership and taking this concept back to your organization, your manager or workplace leader may claim "this won't work here." One of the pitfalls for those that return to their workplace with a concept such as collective leadership, is that they go back with direct ideas and want to have an immediate impact; it is really more about influencing colleagues and stakeholders, rather than preaching collective leadership.

When trying to enact change in a workplace, it is most effective to influence the culture through your own behaviours and make others aware of strengths and weaknesses of the system. This involves providing individuals with the skills to influence managers, stakeholders, and peers, to get them all on-board with a collective leadership approach.

Influencing involves the trained individual being explicitly aware of the existing culture and conforming enough to then gradually deviate. You need to be aware of the current workplace processes and sensitivities, and then prioritize what you want to change within the process and how you want to influence stakeholders. Start with familiarizing yourself on their strategy and what works for them—if you don't understand how and why they work, you can't influence them to work differently.

This requires a lot of empathy—but not the type typically addressed in leadership development. To really change the system, it requires empathy with peers and managers, and making it psychologically safe for them to change their leadership approach.

When we talk about psychological safety, we often talk about employees feeling comfortable to speak-up on an issue or idea they have. However, with senior managers, it is their role to stand by and support current processes and workplace culture. If someone comes in to an organization wanting to make a change, such as implementing collective leadership, the managers response will be to protect current processes and existing habits—as that is often part of their job.

When you come from leadership development training, you also need to make it psychologically safe for stakeholders to start making changes and thinking about how you can make it safe for them to make change. A lot of this involves selling upwards to senior managers and stakeholders, and sideways to peers and colleagues.

A lot of leadership development programs are good at creating individual awareness and contextual awareness about what is going on in the outside world. What is needed to really apply this knowledge in an organization is to have organizational intelligence—understanding how the organization really works, who makes decisions within the company, what does the culture look like, and then linking and connecting these dots.

When trying to implement collective leadership within an organization, you need to alter the workplace culture in a way that does not disrupt what already exists. What often happens is people come back from training and are seen as disruptive and disrespectful towards the organization's history and culture. This leads to a paradox where you need to respect past accomplishments while still enacting change.

Incorporating collective leadership provides benefits that enable an organization to become more adaptive to the external environment. That is something we see many companies doing today as they experience turbulence and huge challenges for which they need to make strategic changes, in response to factors such as climate change and digitalization. A collaborative and collective approach to leadership can ensure organizations cope more flexibly with trends in the external world.

However, what we often observe is that current workplace cultures can be preventing them from making that change. Therefore, the key is to find a bridge between what already exists and where the company needs to go to ensure you stay adaptive to external factors in a way that does not completely paralyse the organization.

Collaborative approach

As well as members within a team collaborating and sharing leadership responsibilities, collective leadership can also involve being more collaborative between teams and departments. Instead of one department seeing an issue they are facing and trying to fix it within their own team, if there is a collective leadership approach, all departments and managers can work together. This brings together different thoughts and ideas for solving problems that might not have been addressed with individual leadership.

A lot of the challenges companies face are so big they need cross-silo collaboration. One individual leader alone cannot effectively solve all the problems their organization will face; it requires a collaboration of leaders. This can even be done across different organizations, not just within organizations.

You can't make a change if you are only aware of your formal organization; you also need to be aware of the invisible parts.

If you want to make a change in the leadership approach of you organization, you need to understand your organization's current structure. On paper, you have the formal organization, outlining the hierarchy of roles. But in reality, there is an informal organization; the invisible part and the true power dynamics of who really makes the decisions, despite the formal hierarchy. At Vlerick, we want to help leaders make a difference and make a change, and you can't make a change if you are only aware of your formal organization; you also need to be aware of the invisible parts.

When it comes to companies and working with clients, we tend to say that we will not only focus on the individual; we want the impact of our programs to be felt throughout the organization and have a ripple effect. We do not believe you can do that by only transforming the individual. Of course, strengthen the individual, but also make them aware of collective dynamics and give them the skills to influence them.

Strengthen the individual, but also make them aware of collective dynamics and give them the skills to influence them.

Coaching for collective change

A good example is that in many leadership development programs, people receive coaching. Often, this is individual coaching where you sit with a coach and think about personal development—we don't really do this. We hold small group coaching session with four or five peers, where we help them work on an individual development plan but also discuss topics of the day and what it says about their work culture and where can they help each other to make a collective impact.

We help them think about their own values, but also reflect on their organization's history and how they fit in, how they might be stopping the organization from growing, how the workplace culture is stopping them from developing. Ensuring you understand the hierarchy and culture of your workplace is how you can best move forward in implementing a newer, collective leadership approach through influence, and reap the benefits.

Katleen De Stobbeleir, is a full professor of leadership at Vlerick Business School. At Vlerick, Katleen heads the 'Centre for Excellence in Leading Adaptive Organizations'. Her work covers the full spectrum of leadership, including: authenticity, the future of work, the growth mindset, psychological safety, hybrid leadership, responsible and inclusive leader transitions and building a feedback climate.

By Donna Kennedy-Glans and James M. Kerr

Winning Businesses Must Tackle Politics

As trust and faith in elected officials continues to diminish many are looking to businesses for leadership. Businesses should expect to be called upon to fill the gaps. While most business leaders are comfortable sharing succinct mission, vision and value statements, the authors encourage more expansive story-telling about the corporate vision as a means to preempt conflict. This includes crafting a vision for a company's culture that accommodates a wide range of people with differing points of

views and an expectation that staff respect each other's differences and look to learn from one another through polite and respectful dialogue.

Corporate leaders need to anticipate both the growing pressure to take a stand on emerging issues, and the backlash. For some businesses, failure to prepare can become an existential crisis. Based on decades of experience guiding corporate leaders through tricky situations, the authors of this article recommend a deeper understanding of the evolving expectations of business leaders in political space and associated risks, and as well, identify proactive steps that can be taken by private sector organizations.

Most business leaders carefully sidestep entanglement in divisive issues—especially, any issues exuding the faintest whiff of politics. Yet the private sector is increasingly being dragged into fraught political space and there is pressure on business leaders to pick a side in emerging and polarizing social issues. When corporate leaders choose to take a stand on a sensitive issue—transgender rights or climate change, for example—these positions can raise the ire of political actors holding different points of view.

Florida Governor Ron DeSantis and others, for example, are pushing back against

There is pressure on business leaders to pick a side in emerging and polarizing social issues

"woke capitalists", even punishing companies that dare to take a contrary stand. And with the risk of global proxy wars turning into hot wars, the to-and-fro between the private and public sectors is likely to remain mutable.

Corporate leaders can no longer avoid the politics

Like it or not, companies play a role in the political process; individual businesses have to be clear about what their role will be and tread carefully. As Disney's CEO Bob Chapek learned the hard way, corporate statements on sensitive issues like transgender rights can be weaponized by one side or the other to further divide and inflame. For those companies that choose to play a role in finding solutions to hot-button issues, explicit and ongoing conversations with like-minded stakeholders and corporate critics are essential to map out when and how and why their company will take a political stand. These are corporate stories that need to be told, preferably as a pre-emptive strategy and not in reaction to crisis.

Discerning all of the potential landmines within a complex, emotionally-charged terrain is not easy for companies; Coca-Cola's reaction to the divisive Black Lives Matter movement is illustrative. In the wake of George Floyd's death in June 2020, Coca-Cola acknowledged the company's duty to Black people in America, echoing the corporation's response nearly thirty years earlier when Rodney King was beaten by police. Coca-Cola positioned itself in the Black Lives Matter debate in a very deliberate way, through collaboration with like-minded advocates.

But in 2021, the company hit a political wall when activists, customers and a powerful coalition of Black executives pressured Coca-Cola to take a stand in opposing legislation advanced by Republicans in the State of Georgia to restrict voting access. This expectation was a step outside of the company's comfort zone and their executive team declined to take a partisan position, precipitating calls for boycotts of Coca-Cola's products. After the legislation was signed into law, the company pledged to *"work to advance voting rights and access in Georgia and across the country."* For many, this promise was too little, too late.

Further, the Walt Disney Company faced a similar quandary. Disney's initial strategy—to keep out of the spotlight and remain silent during the debate on Florida's "Don't Say Gay" bill—triggered a barrage of criticism from employees and the LGBTQ+ community. In response, Disney CEO Bob Chapek publicly apologized: *"I missed the mark in this case but am an ally you can count on—and I will be an outspoken champion for the protections, visibility, and opportunity you deserve."*

Florida Governor Ron DeSantis, a Republican, agreed to meet with Chapek but publicly questioned the role of companies in sensitive public policy debates: *"And so in Florida, our policies got to be based on the best interest of Florida citizens, not on the musing of woke corporations."* Things got worse when lawmakers in Florida revoked Disney World's designation as a special tax district, a privilege the company has held for fifty-five years.

Discerning all of the potential landmines within a complex, emotionally-charged terrain is not easy for companies

More recently, Republican state treasurers in the United States are deploying strategies to punish businesses that they believe are unduly focused on environmental issues. The treasurer of West Virginia used a new state law to ban five financial firms (Morgan Stanley, Wells Fargo, Goldman Sachs, JP Morgan and BlackRock) from doing business in West Virginia because the companies were backing away from fossil fuels.

It's impossible to predict where this will all end. And on top of all this domestic tension building between the public and private sectors, there is a war in Ukraine and nervousness about Taiwan that could force corporate leaders to become entangled in global politics. What unfolded in Russia in the early part of 2022 was unprecedented. Hundreds of global businesses voluntarily suspended their operations in that country, in response to President Vladimir Putin's invasion of Ukraine. In the absence of legal sanctions, companies as diverse as McDonalds, BP, Harley-Davidson, Amazon, Baker Botts, Deloitte, Starbucks, and 3M simply walked away. These decisions were not virtue-signaling, public-relations gestures. There were immediate, direct and significant financial, operational and reputation consequences for these businesses.

Things have changed. Forty years ago, there was not a rush of global businesses exiting from operations in apartheid South Africa. Legal sanctions were debated, but often got caught up in partisan tangles. Conservative political leaders at that time, including British Prime Minister Margaret Thatcher

and U.S. President Ronald Reagan, preferred "constructive engagement" to divestment. John Major, Thatcher's Foreign Secretary, then said divestment would "feed white consciences outside South Africa, not black bellies within it." Global companies faced stern anti-apartheid advocacy, often led by faith leaders using the language of morality, yet for many years, companies that chose to remain invested in South Africa had political cover. General Motors, then the largest employer of Blacks in apartheid South Africa, did not divest until 1986.

Start by imagining the possibilities. Ask a very basic question: "What can this company become?"

Many corporate leaders we have worked with prefer to not get entangled in anything remotely political for fear of being tainted, co-opted or compromised. Yet it is nearly impossible to run a business today without rubbing up against politics. As companies pulling out of investments in Russia or facing the censure of Republican politicians are learning in real time, there may be times when you have no choice but to take a political stand. Your company does not want to become a lightning rod for powerful critics and it is also very difficult to manage an organization in crisis-response mode. How can your organization navigate this fraught space with greater confidence?

We have some ideas for you to prepare your organization, preserve your business and provide stability that may be missing.

Take a proactive step to help your company weather the torm

Most business leaders are familiar with the design of succinct mission, vision and value statements; while necessary, we are suggesting that these tired and uninspired statements that appear on corporate websites and stream from corporate rafters are not sufficient.

You know the ones: *"We value diversity and inclusion."*

Or *"We're dedicated to being stewards of Planet Earth and we'll do whatever it takes to ensure our operations and investments are managed in ways that reduce negative ecological and environmental impacts."*

Or: *"We are passionate about understanding and responding to customer needs for privacy. Our technology-based solutions operate across key stages of our customers' work flow. Our products are demonstrably superior to our competitors."*

These kinds of corporate statements read like *motherhood and apple pie*—pleasant and easy to digest but not all that distinctive. These statements do not describe the company or what it is like to be part of the organization. They do not serve to distinguish a specific enterprise because they could apply to nearly any company within the industry. And they provide little guidance or insight to internal or external stakeholders trying to figure out what your company's approach might be to an emerging challenge—including diversity, de-carbonization or privacy— all issues with a wide range of perspectives.

This is why we advise companies to craft a 'Vision Story'—a more fulsome story with depth to explain not just 'the what?' of your organization but 'the how?' and 'the why?'. We encourage the creation of a corporate Vision Story to supplement corporate mission, vision and value statements, a story so compelling and vivid that the average working professional wants to be part of your organization. Here is how to begin.

Constructing a compelling Vision Story

Above all else, a Vision Story must be engaging. Corporate employees and other key stakeholders must be able to see themselves in the story. Futuristic in its tone and loose and sinuous in its organization, a Vision Story is written as if the company has already completed the work needed to achieve its vision. Typically, fifteen to twenty pages in length, the story must include a detailed discussion of what a company is to become in order to achieve its long-range goals. It is an aspirational document.

How do you begin? Start by imagining the possibilities. Ask a very basic question: "What can this company become?"

Inevitably, the initial answers will set stretch financial goals, like, "We will be at $100 billion by 2024," or "We will operate at a 40% margin by 2025." A strong statement of the financial goals often frames the Vision Story. People want to understand how ambitious a company aims to be and financial measures act as a differentiator among options (for example, a company may be described as "small and growing"; "mid-sized and specialized"; or "large and dominant").

But these financial aspirations are just the beginning of the story. In the rest of the Vision Storytelling, describe where the company wants to be in the future in relation to these four elements:

1. **Corporate values** (e.g., integrity, diversity and inclusion, social responsibility, carbon reduction, respect for privacy);
2. **Corporate strategies** (i.e., general tactics for gaining competitive advantage, driving innovation, extending geographic reach);
3. **Corporate governance** (e.g., frameworks for decision-making, communication, community engagement); and
4. **Management structures** (e.g., organizational design, operating models and leadership responsibilities).

Interestingly, Disney has this mission statement on its website: *"The mission of The Walt Disney Company is to entertain, inform and inspire people around the globe through the power of unparalleled storytelling, reflecting the iconic brands, creative minds and innovative technologies that make ours the world's premier entertainment company."*

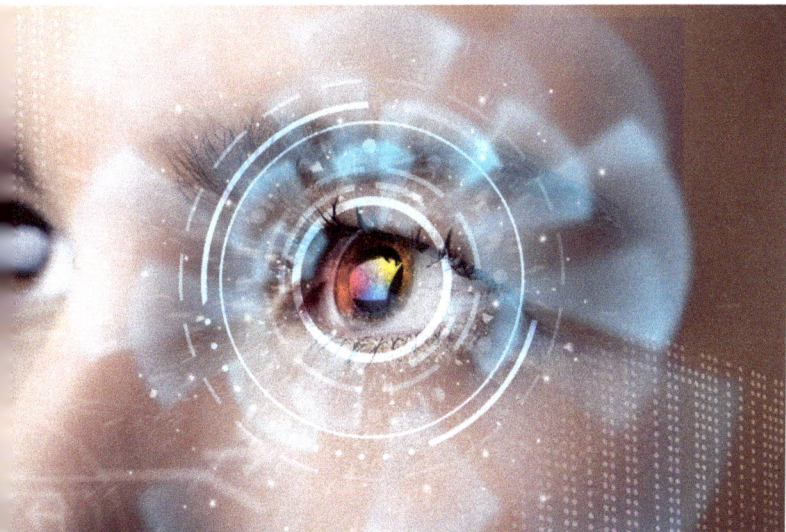

However, it doesn't have a story that explains where it's heading, who works there, what they do, who they do it for and what matters most when their people are delivering products and services to its varied customer-base. This is a glaring flaw in its strategic thinking, in our opinion. After all, according to Disney, its strength is *"unparalleled storytelling."*

Considering that a well-crafted Vision Story can help to pre-empt conflict, whether generated from within (from leadership and staff) or from without (customers, special interest groups, politicians, etc.), because it can articulate the values on which the business is built. For example, Disney's vision story might include a passage like this:

"Our culture accommodates a wide range of people with differing points of views. While we don't expect our staff to embrace any one set of ideas, we do expect our staff to respect each other's differences and look to learn from each other

A Vision Story is only as good as the level of commitment manifested by an organization's stakeholders

through polite and respectful dialogue. We don't want to ostracize, or otherwise punish those who don't think like us. Rather, we strive to create a work environment that encourages each person to bring their best selves to work each day in service of our customers."

In other words, Disney is making it clear that it does not tell its people what to think. Instead, it is committed to allowing the space for uncomfortable conversations and if necessary, providing the training needed to teach its people how to share different points of view, respectfully. Had Disney put a Vision Story in place, it could have easily pointed to it when it was coming under attack for being "too woke" for Florida's Governor.

'Walking the talk' is essential

Indeed, a Vision Story is only as good as the level of commitment manifested by an organization's stakeholders, as it is these stakeholders that will be held accountable for any behaviours, actions and, dare we say, crimes that stain an organization in the view of the general public.

Sure, there may be times when the company does decide it needs to take a stand on a political or polarized issue (carbon reduction targets, for example), but, will only do so after careful consideration of its impact on its employees and key stakeholders.

SAMSUNG

Thank you to those fighting for our lives

Coca-Cola

together we must

start change
demand justice
end racism

BLACK LIVES MATTER

Times Square, New York - Xackery Irving / Shutterstock

Get ahead of conflict by daring to talk about these questions pre-emptively

By way of illustration, Disney's could easily include a discussion of its corporate culture, which aims to create a *"big tent"* that accommodates and respects divergent tastes and differing points of view. Clearly, this would signal that Disney recognizes that its employees, customers, suppliers and other members of its ecosystem have different perspectives on sensitive social questions including abortion, transgender rights, and climate change. While the company does not necessarily choose to take a stand on any of these social issues, its Vision Story suggests that it is committed to creating a safe space within the company for respectful dialogue among internal and external stakeholders on these questions.

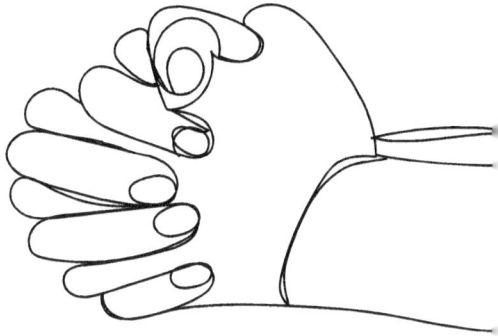

One last point, your organization's Vision Story should also anticipate the possibility that your company's perspective on a controversial or polarized social issue may attract unwanted attention from critics (for example, champions of anti-woke or woke capitalism; climate change deniers or crusaders). It is easier to envision how your organization will collaborate with like-minded and fair-minded stakeholders to build alliances and shared messages (much as Coca-Cola did with the Black Lives Matter campaign), but how will your organization respond when you face a barrage of criticism from influential political actors, special interest groups or consumers?

Many organizations do not fare well in these kinds of situations and it is tempting to capitulate under pressure. A fully-formed Vision Story equips you to anticipate this possibility and creates the space to find a path forward in a time of crisis. Of course, your organization will need allies to sustain your point of view and withstand opposition but you will also require a deliberate corporate strategy.

Businesses that take care in developing strong Vision Stories are more successful in managing crises than ones that fail to do so.

Final thoughts

Indeed, the crafting of a Vision Story is reflective work. It is important to get your team in a relaxed frame of mind. Drafting these stories, or even excerpts, rarely works well in a crisis. Encourage your team to sit back, close their eyes, and clear their minds of the clutter that can sometime consume us as we go about our work day. It is all about imagining the company's shared future, together.

It is worth the effort. Businesses that take care in developing strong Vision Stories—stories that clearly articulate where the organization will be in the future and how it will get there—are in our experience more successful in managing crises than ones that fail to do so. After all, how do you know you have arrived if you don't know where you want to be!

Corporate leaders should expect unrelenting pressure for their company to take a position on controversial issues. Employees, customers, investors, suppliers and host communities where your company operates are likely to have strongly held opinions on the company's position and best strategy. Get ahead of conflict by daring to talk about these questions pre-emptively, through the crafting of a corporate Vision Story.

Pro-forma statements—on values, mission and corporate vision—are essential but they are not sufficient. Companies need to dig deeper to imagine how they prefer that their organization handles emerging controversies, and expectations about their corporate role in finding solutions to these problems. In the heat of a crisis, there is often little time or emotional capacity for the kinds of conversations required to identify effective approaches.

In the past, the public may not have expected the private sector to assume such a direct role in solving pressing social, environmental and governance challenges. Individual companies will have to decide what role they can play to help fill the void, and provide some stability in very uncertain times.

James M. Kerr *is a sought-after consultant, coach, keynote speaker and author with 6 popular business books to his credit. He was named a Global Gurus Top 30 Thought Leader and a Thinkers360 Top 10 Leadership Thinker in 2022. His popular podcast The Indispensable Conversation is known for its provocative business ideas and insights. Reach him at* jim@indispensable-consulting.com

Donna Kennedy-Glans, LLB, QC, Author of Teaching the Dinosaur to Dance: Moving Beyond Business as Usual (2022) and Corporate Integrity: A Toolkit for Managing beyond Compliance (Wiley, 2005). Donna has 30+ years of experience in the global energy sector, working on projects in over 35 countries then served as an elected politician and cabinet minister in Canada. Reach her at dkennedyglans@shaw.ca

CURATION

PORTABILITY

C
A
S
C
A
D
I
G

Enhance risk

Future
skills

Job mobility

Investment

Credentialing

By Daniel Chadwick

Lifelong Learning and University-Based Business Schools

An Executive Summary of a Report from IEDP for AACSCB and UNICON

Organizations globally continue to need constant development of their people to evolve and grow their businesses. The eco-system of executive education is increasingly complex, with more players and more participants seeking the best solutions for themselves and their clients. We present here the key takeaways from a significant report published earlier this year by IEDP in association with AACSCB, the leading global business school association, and UNICON, the global consortium of business school based executive education organizations.

For university-based business schools a potential pivot towards lifelong learning is a strategic question many are grappling with.

Earlier this year IEDP.com conducted qualitative interviews with a range of voices from the supply and demand sides of executive education—from deans and presidents of business schools to directors and heads of executive education, and CLOs and heads of talent at large organizations. These in-depth interviews were with field experts in their relevant roles at: Goldman Sachs, Volkswagen Group, New York Life, Hyatt Hotels, TBWA, Pitney Bowes, and Cargill, on the demand side; Leeds Illuminate and the Financial Times as key cross-sector observers; and IMD, INSEAD, Tsinghua University, UVA Darden Executive Education & Lifelong Learning, Michigan Ross, Columbia Business School, Illinois Tech, and IE University, on the supply side. In addition to this qualitative data the report leverages a wide research sweep, with supporting quantitative data and insights gathered from a wide range of trusted sources, from WEF, to Deloitte, McKinsey, PwC, Carrington Crisp, and others—along with AACSB's and UNICON's own research.

Executive Summary – In Brief

We are at a time when the status quo across business education is being challenged. Traditional, front-loaded educational models—with funding and time investment skewed towards the 18-24 age bracket, and with skills updated all-too-rarely subsequent to that—were even five years ago a product no longer meeting the needs of the customer, nor the wider needs of employers and industries. A variety of disruptive market forces now pose long-term, strategic questions for higher-ed leaders, executive education teams, and corporate talent leaders to evaluate and explore. For university-based business schools a potential pivot towards lifelong learning is a strategic question many are grappling with. Such a move will require new products, new services, new business models, and new technologies, which in turn require time, effort, and financial investment to get right—therefore key decisions lie ahead. To guide and support the strategizing required at this important juncture, AACSB, IEDP, and UNICON have partnered together to produce this research report and make it available to decision-makers across executive education. The full report comprises a deep-dive SWOT analysis of the strengths, weaknesses, opportunities, and threats presented by lifelong learning as a driver and shaper of future business strategy for the sector. The aim for this initiative is to provide substantive research for stakeholders in executive education to feed into their own decision-making processes, and ultimately to play a role in improving the impact of executive education in the round—which is a shared goal of AACSB, IEDP, and UNICON. In this executive summary you will find a distilled, concise version of the SWOT analysis, as well as key takeaways for readers to take forward in their own work and thinking in this area.

Takeaways

This SWOT analysis study reinforces some pre-existing views around lifelong learning already widely held within business school circles— namely that there is an outdated status quo in executive education; that it is ripe for disruption; and that

The demand now is for flexible, lower-cost access to knowledge and skills, updated regularly on a career-long continuum

the ideas and principles of lifelong learning offer a compelling framework around which new solutions and strategies may be built, to better serve both the supply and demand sides of the industry. – More valuably, by asking eminent voices from all sides of the sector to focus on the potential strengths, weaknesses, opportunities, and threats posed by this approach, the research has collected a deep set of new insights, reflections, and provocations for decision-makers to feed into their own strategizing and support the formulation of new solutions. – From this research we can generate takeaways from the perspectives of each of the three main stakeholder groups addressed here; corporate learning and talent leaders, business school and university leaders, and executive education leaders.

TAKEAWAYS FOR CORPORATES

• The work and skills landscape has drastically changed what executives require from their learning. The demand now is for flexible, lower-cost access to knowledge and skills, updated regularly on a career-long continuum. Individuals and organizations desire learning that is supplied just-in-time, to deploy across projects and other short-term time horizons.

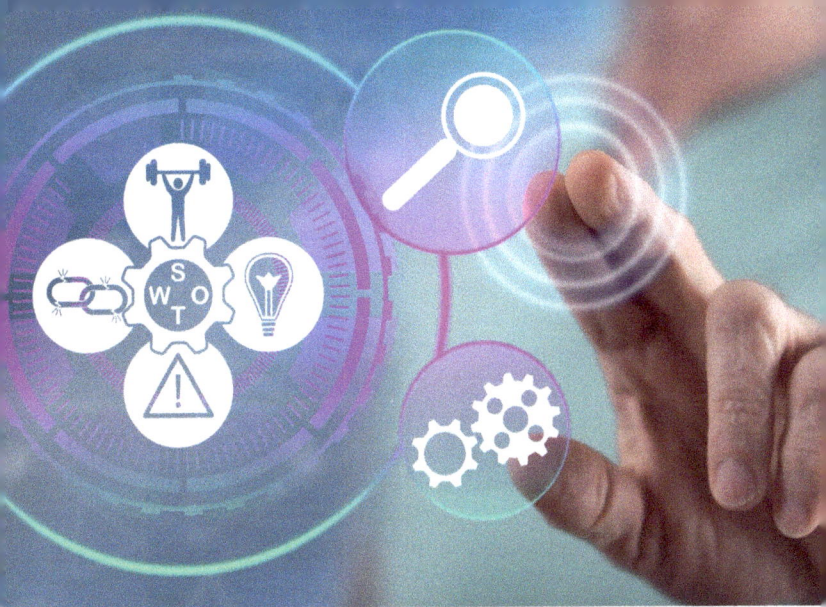

- Higher turnover rates, fluid career trajectories, and the 'war to retain talent', now make reskilling, rebooting, and reinventing careers—multiple times over during one's lifetime—increasingly the norm. The scale of demand is therefore massive, with talent functions increasingly widening focus to include hitherto less-represented segments of the organization.

- Currently the term itself 'lifelong learning' has little to no cut-through in the corporate world and is not a recognized solution to these new challenges and requirements. Where lifelong learning solutions are emerging, tensions are at play— such as balancing rising demand for personalized learning with a drive to deliver learning at scale; and the challenge of aligning personal goals with organizational goals.

- This research indicates that corporate talent leaders such as CLOs are quick to adopt the best new technologies available to them and happy to give new providers and players a chance to deliver results and excellence. They are typically confident in their ability to build internal solutions, integrating new technologies, and innovating to meet changing needs.

- With increased choice of providers, suppliers, and practitioners to partner with, and the increased availability of high-quality content—talent leaders are, more so than ever, designers and curators of their own corporate learning agendas, rather than simply 'buyers' in the marketplace.

- These developments make the demand side of the market more exacting and results-driven than ever. By the same token, talent leaders are also better informed than ever, making them highly intelligent and responsive partners for providers to work closely with to achieve results.

- Business schools are viewed as being an astute, logical, and trustworthy choice for the provision of lifelong learning— though with some caveats applied: namely around an existing market impression of business school education as sometimes 'heavy' i.e. intricate, time-consuming, and expensive—which was seen to be at odds with lifelong learning's appeal.

TAKEAWAYS FOR BUSINESS SCHOOLS
- Business school and university leaders play a critical role as custodians of the wider institution's brand values, and insurers of the institutions continuing market trust, excel-

Talent leaders are now designers and curators of their own corporate learning agendas, rather than simply 'buyers' in the marketplace

lence, and credentialling power. As business school leaders they are also the decision-makers best placed to address the structural and cultural questions posed by the potential adoption of lifelong learning as a strategy—which may require a large-scale, top-down change effort in many cases. Many of the areas of such a change, are typically controlled at the wider business school level—research agenda, faculty training, teaching capacity, spending power, investment, and much more.

- A key tension at play for business school leaders is around research. Faculty research is both a unique selling point for the business school (with non-traditional providers unlikely to compete at a comparable level)—but it may also serve as a source of impediment and resistance—from the costliness of research production, to a lack of speed and agility to meet new trends.

- Another tension is around lifelong learning viewed as being in opposition to traditional degree learning. Many flexible learning solutions such as micro-credentials do seek to deconstruct longer form degree learning—however, are these products necessarily tied to the future existence of degree learning? We might conclude that by virtue of the differing audiences, and the scale and demographic of demand—that they could instead be seen as complimentary.

- University-based business schools possess high degrees of convening power, offering a learning 'destination' that non-traditional providers tend not to. They also sit across a wide variety of knowledge and research, positioning them to offer cross-discipline and career-long learning solutions, as well as give up-to-the-minute expertise on technologies and themes pertinent to the future of work.

TAKEAWAYS FOR EXECUTIVE EDUCATION

- The executive education unit within a business school has long been viewed as the entrepreneurial arm to the academic institution—most likely to innovate and deliver new revenues through their strong connections to the corporate market and typically commercially-minded teams and leaders.

- This research confirms these units as well-placed to take a lead in the area of lifelong learning. Executive education teams possess deep expertise around the science of learning; they partner closely with their corporate clients to focus on impact and value creation; many have, in recent years, demonstrated a willingness to pivot and adopt online learning as a core capability; and they are purpose-driven in their belief that learning can improve societal as well as business outcomes.

- The primary challenges for executive education lie around the scale of change and investment required, and the structural impediments in their relationship with the wider business school and university, which may hinder agility and/or appetite to challenge the status quo. At a more granu-

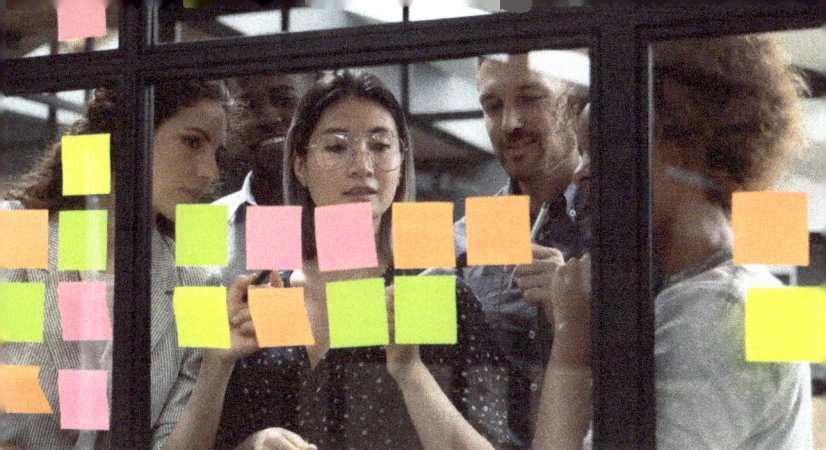

lar level, this research highlights a key challenge around connecting the personal goals inherent in lifelong learning, with wider, strategic organizational goals for employers.

- Other concerns include the potential reliance on self-directed learning, which has been shown to favour only the most engaged learners, as well as the risk that some providers will use the term lifelong learning as a slogan only, as opposed to a meaningful, action-based strategy. – The greatest opportunities for executive education lie around the scale of demand, and the ability to be market-driven to tap into it— finding new market segments and cascading out to new learner profiles, and generating new revenue streams as a result.

What next?

Many leaders and practitioners on all sides of the executive learning are already trialling, piloting, and working on solutions that better meet the modern skills and employability needs of organizations and individual learners. Some providers are further along in this process and may be viewed as positive case studies in the field:

The University of Virginia's Darden School of Business is an example of putting lifelong learning front and centre—renaming and rebranding their executive education offering 'Darden Executive Education & Lifelong Learning'; restructuring leadership around the rebrand; and committing to build a new Sands Institute of Lifelong Learning to continue to innovate in the non-degree space.

The University of Michigan's Ross School of Business' 'Alumni Advantage' program is an example of a business school leveraging their considerable, international alumni network to offer learning and networking benefits to their alumni, offering continued value above and beyond the original degree-focused relationship.

The Haas School of Business is an example of an executive education unit developing a stellar brand reputation of its own, able to operate independently, whilst still enjoying the wider associations of its parent institution, UC Berkeley. Under the leadership of Rich Lyons, Dean of the Haas School from 2008 to 2018, the Haas school quadrupled the size of its executive education unit in ten years, and more than quadrupled the contribution of executive education to the school's bottom-line.

BI Norwegian Business School is an example of demand-led program development. The school launched a range of short, stackable online learning modules during the pandemic, in response to the changing requirements and knowledge upskilling needs of their audience. The new portfolio of short digital courses attracted more than 5000 participants in the first 19 months, with the platform enabling innovation around new business concepts and new pedagogy for the "new normal" in work and education life.

The reskilling drive in China provides intriguing examples of partnerships and collaboration between industry and academia that seek to address the gaps between needed and available skills. From a recent McKinsey report, "Alibaba Group and Hangzhou Normal University co-founded the Alibaba Business School, which offers four bachelor's degrees. DJI, a commercial drone maker, launched a joint innovation laboratory with the Hong Kong University of Science and Technology to drive further advances in unmanned aerial vehicle technology." [Source: McKinsey Global Institute Report, 'Reskilling China: Transforming the world's largest workforce into lifelong learners', January, 2021]

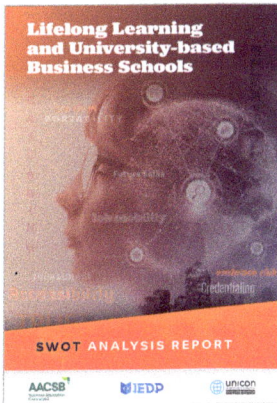

This article has been drawn from the Executive Summary of the 'Lifelong Learning and University-based Business Schools' Report which can be accessed here: **www.iedp.com/media/4660/aacsb-iedp-unicon-ll-swot-executive_summary-final.pdf**

Read the Full Report here: **www.iedp.com/media/4659/aacsb-iedp-unicon-ll-swot-full_report-final.pdf**

By Paul Brown

Refining the Solution to an Emotional Muddle

O ne of the curious things about the 20th century is how much that century was dominated by psychology as a way of trying to make sense of human behaviour in all its manifest idiosyncrasies. Two decades on, some hindsight observations about psychology might be pertinent.

Psychology likes to define itself as 'the science of human behaviour' or 'the science of the mind'. But a little thought about what a true science is might raise a question as to whether either of those claims is true.

Galileo risked burning at the stake for challenging the mediaeval church's Aristotelian view that the earth was the centre of the universe; but even if he had to deny what he knew to be true in order to avoid the horrors of being burned to death, suffering a 15-year house imprisonment instead, he laid the foundations of a modern science that Isaac Newton especially built on. Following the ten-year English Civil War that ended in 1651 and that resulted in nine years of the only period in English history of non-monarchical rule, Charles II was restored to the throne in 1660. There was then an extraordinary flowering of the arts, science and fashion; of which one manifestation was the founding of what is now known as The Royal Society – the oldest and pre-eminent scientific society in the world and in which being elected a Fellow is the highest mark of recognition among the worldwide scientific community.

But what is special about science? It is that there is agreement, backed by replicable experimental evidence, of what one is observing or talking about. In so far as facts can ever be true, science relies upon established experimental truths. In distinction, other bodies of knowledge – philosophy and theology especially from mediaeval times to this day – rely upon assertion and the individual's belief in their own rightness, but with no underlying proof. The modern social sciences suffer the same dilemma.

Twentieth century psychology fails the test of being a true science. Curiously psychologists across the Western world have never got together, at any stage of their knowledge, to agree fundamental concepts like: What do we mean by 'a person'? or what is 'the Self'? There is a vast literature on both subjects, but it is a contentious literature, not one founded on any starting agreements. And so different psychologists have different answers to such basic questions.

Imagine the chaos if different engineers chose to design bridges based solely on some attribute like design without reference to the inherent properties of metal in suspended arches. When an aeroplane falls out of the sky or a bridge collapses, immense resources are put into discovering why. When a politician fails through what used to be called charac-

In so far as facts can ever be true, science relies upon established experimental truths. In distinction, other bodies of knowledge – philosophy and theology rely upon assertion and the individual's belief in their own rightness, but with no underlying proof. The modern social sciences suffer the same dilemma

ter defects – Nixon, Clinton, Trump, Johnson – no systematic enquiry is made as to how such an event could be foreseen or prevented for the future as there is no replicable science by which to arrive at conclusions.

Let's get such wide concerns down to organizational interests. Leaders, line managers and especially HR in organizations seriously lack a considered and agreed framework within which to define and understand those extraordinary assets – people – without whom no organization could exist at all.

This piece is to highlight one especially contentious issue and offer a working solution that might form the basis of an enlarged understanding of some aspects of human, and especially organizational, behaviour. For the modern brain-sciences, having direct access to the workings of the brain in the way that psychologists never have had, are telling us that we human beings are essentially *energy* systems and not, primarily, psychological systems. It is not difficult to move from that observation to an understanding that the pursuit of strategic

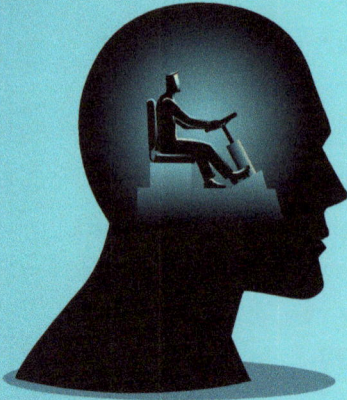

> *What the 21st century brain sciences have shown us is that our thinking system is there to give us an account of what our brain already knows*

and operational goals, organizationally, must rely on the way human energy has been applied – or mis-applied – within the organization.

There are many words used socially as well as organizationally as if they were commonly understood. The complex word 'emotions' is one, with its attendant concepts of 'feelings', 'moods' and 'states'. No-one denies their existence, but what exactly are they? Psychology has certainly not agreed a working definition, but the modern brain-sciences are showing us how they work.

'Emotions' tend to get a bad press in organizations. But if one hyphenates the word as e-motion it is suddenly possible to see that embedded in it is the fact that energy produces action. Stated descriptively as $e=m^2$, a new formulation for organizational behaviour appears. The energy of the emotions underpins action and motivational focus.

The 17th century philosopher Descartes coined the phrase that translates as 'I think, therefore I am'. As the precursor to the 18th century Enlightenment in the Western world it created a split between the 'rational' and the 'irrational'; with a strong implication that the first was much preferable to the second because the second was emotional. 120 years of psychology has not re-integrated the two. In general, psychology consigned 'the emotions' to the darker side of human experience in a place difficult to access called 'the unconscious' which, when attached to the Freudian concepts of repressed sexual desires, made 'the emotions' a place to avoid unless explored in the privacy of the psychoanalytic couch.

But two changes have happened in this 21st century that create the opportunity for a new framework of understanding about the emotions. And if, as they do, they drive behaviour, then a more precise understanding of them is crucial for the post-Covid better development and re-think of the distributed interdependence that has been forced upon all organizations.

The first change is that Freud has been shown to be something of a fraud. In much of his writing, he described clinical material that fitted his theories but, it transpires, the clinical material was fabricated for the purposes of supporting his theories. In a page-turner of a book, *Freud: the making of an illusion,* author Frederick Crews describes the detective work he did on previously inaccessible archival material in divining what Freud was really up to.

The second change, and of huge significance, is now that the modern brain-sciences are showing us that we human beings are, like the rest of the physical world, essentially energy systems, and that what we have generally called our 'psychology' is the product of the way the brain has organized itself via the emotional system as experience, coupled to genetics

We do not think our way through life... we feel our way, and then give ourselves a cognitive account of that

coupled to neurochemistry. This makes each of us who we are, and the primary task of the brain is to both organize and manage that process. So, our individuality, character, personality, or – to wrap those up in one much-over-used 20th century word, our 'psychology', comes into being and is sustained via the emotional system. It is what makes each of us the unique individual that we each are.

We come into the world, day one, not only with the neurochemistry of our mother's lived experiences having shaped our brains *in utero* whilst interacting with the designs of XX (female) or XY (male) chromosomes, but with the life-long potential for assimilating and recording and then enlarging and living off experience. That experience is encoded by the basic emotions in complex patterns within the 86 billion brain cells that we each possess. Attached eventually to language, that is the mechanism by which we create meaning. What the 21st century brain sciences have shown us is that our thinking system is there to give us an account of what our brain already knows, driven as it is by our own internal meaning-making derived from our own life experience. We do not think our way through life, even though we might think we do! We *feel* our way, and then give ourselves a cognitive account of that - which makes us think we are rational. The emotional system is not irrational, though. We now know it has its own rule base.

What an understanding of human behaviour lacks from the vantage point of the modern brain-sciences is a working model of the primary or basic emotions that gives thinkers about organizational behaviour a common starting point in studying or mobilizing 'the emotions.' In a wider context, it is of concern that, in research on the emotions, neuroscience labs around the world are in danger of adopting a variety of starting points based on various propositions emanating from social psychology about 'the emotions', creating what looks like scientific literature but proves to be one that defies comparative analysis because of the differing starting points.

The Eight Basic Emotions

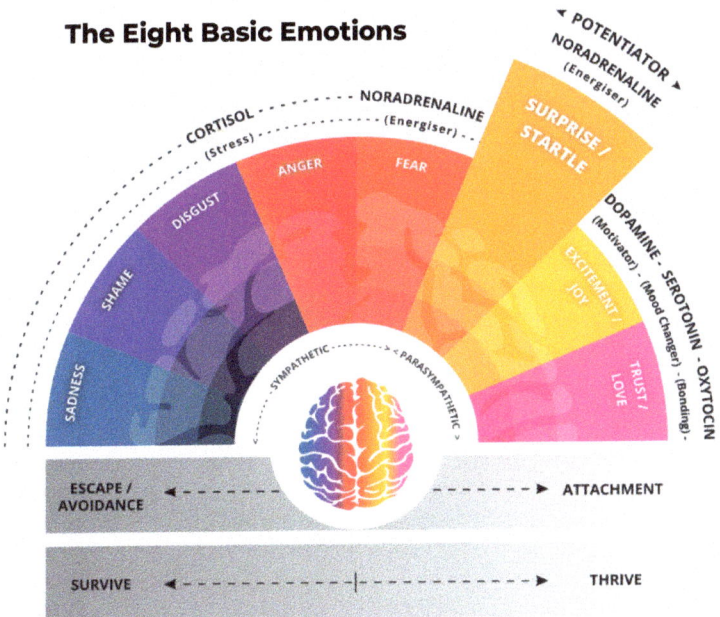

The London Protocol of the Emotions - v.2
©2020 Professor P T Brown

'Moods' are difficult to understand and define, as they contain within them an energy that transmits to others for which there is as yet no adequate physical explanation.

A synthesis of a great deal of literature has produced the following proposal as a means of having a shared common starting point for what, in practice, is meant by 'the emotions.' It is believed to be the only attempt in the literature on the emotions to propose this shared common starting point and, in a single display, to specify the emotions on a continuum from escape/avoidance through to attachment; and to specify a survive – thrive dimension; and to link them at the same time to the basic neurochemicals and the commonly-understood behaviours arising from the sympathetic and parasympathetic nervous system reactions. It is a development of a proposal first put forward in 2018

In an artist's palette, three primary colours are variously mixed to create the whole of the colour range used. All great paintings have the same basic materials but are all different. So, it is with us human beings. In response to the stimuli of experience the eight basic emotions combine to create the complexity of the feeling system that underpins all our behaviours, choices and decisions.

The emotional system also has the capacity to create moods and states. 'Moods' are difficult to understand and define, as they contain within them an energy that transmits to others for which there is as yet no adequate physical expla-

nation. Moods are palpable. The mood of a boss defines for many people the fundamental conditions of their working day's experience.

'States' are combinations of the emotions that imply inner awareness of experience without there being any specific, goal-directed behaviours resulting. 'Happiness', for example, is a state. States can be observed empathetically by others, but they do not have the same capacity to infect or hijack another's emotional system in the way that moods do. Whether or not, as the US Declaration of Independence would have it, the pursuit of happiness as an inalienable right is of any particular value to a nation is open to question. It was perhaps best reformulated by the great Vietnamese monk, Thich Nhat Hanh, when he observed that:

There is no way to happiness: happiness is the way.

In summary, then, neuroscience lacks any agreed understanding of what 'the emotions' are, 20th century psychology having contentiously failed to establish any such agreement. But it is now clear, through the modern brain-sciences, that the emotional system both shapes and organizes the pathways of the developing brain and controls all subsequent behaviour. It is proposed that the London Protocol of the Emotions synthesizes current knowledge in such a way that, if line managers and especially HR were to become fluent in its implications, it forms the basis for a widely understood starting point that lifts a working understanding of the emotions out of the shadows of knowledge into the light of understood organizational use.

Dr Paul Brown is a clinical and organizational psychologist, Professor of Organisational Neuroscience at Monarch Business School Switzerland and Visiting Professor at Henley Business School UK. He is Chairman of ION Consulting International in Singapore and lives in Lao PDR.

Reader Offer – Online Program on 'Brain and Behaviour in Organizations'

If you are interested in furthering your understanding of how emotions impact organizational behaviour, Prof Brown, with Ideas for Leaders, has created an eight-module online program on **Brain and Behaviour in Organizations**. You can enrol for it at **programs.ideasforleaders.com/p/brain-and-behaviour-in-organisations** or by using the QR code below.

Developing Leaders Quarterly readers can apply a 25% discount to the program cost by using the **DLQ0922** discount code.

IDEAS FOR LEADERS

Academic research in
accessible and engaging
bite-sized chunks

LEARNING POWER: LEARNERS MUST TAKE CONTROL

KEY CONCEPT

A new model of learning power, based on 15 years of data, emphasizes the responsibility that individuals must take for their own learning. The new model unveils the complex relationships among the learning power dimensions, from mindful agency (self-determination and initiative) to openness to learning to relationship dimensions such as collaboration and belonging.

IDEA SUMMARY

Based on extensive research, the Effective Lifelong Learning Inventory was developed in the late 1990s as an assessment tool for learning power. Specifically, the ELLI model identified seven qualities or dimensions necessary for learning: the five 'active' learning power dimensions of strategic awareness, creativity, curiosity, meaning making and changing and learning; the learning relationships dimension; and the fragility and dependence dimension. The results of the assessment could be graphed in a seven-spoke 'spidergram'.

The relationships among the seven dimensions remained unexplored. Over the past several years, one of the original developers of ELLI, University of Bristol's Ruth Deakin Crick, and several of her colleagues have revisited the metrics in the assessment tool, taking into consideration the developing research (including her own), as well as the new data accumulated since the original model was developed.

Focusing on the role of purpose in learning — which includes taking responsibility for learning purposes, processes and procedures — Crick and her team changed the name of the original 'strategic awareness' dimension to mindful agency.

'Agency' refers to the extent that one has control of an event. Mindful agency thus refers to a learner's inclination or ability to want to learn and to take steps to learn. In this perspective, the other active dimensions — creativity, curiosity and the renamed sense-making and hope and optimism — are supporting players of mindful agency.

The team then turned its attention to the two remaining dimensions of the original model: 'learning relationships' and 'fragility and dependence'.

Learning relationships, their analysis showed, consisted of three latent variables: collaborating with others, belonging to a learned community, and dependency. Collaborating and belonging are positive approaches to learning, while dependency is a state of being. For that reason, Crick identified collaborating and belonging as two new dimensions of learning. The dependency factor was relegated to the last remaining dimension of the original assessment: fragility and dependence.

Originally, a low score on fragility and dependence was interpreted as resilience. But new analysis showed that this dimension was much more complicated. Both high and low levels of fragility and dependence can result in learners closing themselves off from learning opportunities. Therefore, the dimension was changed to openness to learning.

Instead of seven independent dimensions, the new learning power model explains how its eight updated dimensions interrelate. In metaphorical terms, the original model offered its seven dimensions as ingredients on a list. The new model offers its eight dimensions as the working parts of an engine.

At the heart of the engine's operation is mindful agency, to which creativity, curiosity, sense-making and optimism and hope contribute; mindful agency interacts with the openness to learning dimension, and both mindful agency and openness to learning interact with the two relationship dimensions, belonging and collaboration..

BUSINESS APPLICATION

Leaders todays recognize that internal motivation — the kind that emerges when people love their work and believe it is important — is more effective in inspiring superior performance than external motivation that depends on financial incentive or top-down commands.

This learning power model thus fits into contemporary attitudes about engaging and motivating people. Learning occurs through the regulation of information flow and energy. This model recognizes that how much information flows to and from the learner, and how much energy the learner puts into the process, is dependent on the individual. Mindful agency is about having the confidence and self-awareness to want to learn, and taking the steps necessary to learn.

At the same time leaders (and peers) can play a role in helping learners achieve their learning purpose. For example, leaders can:

- Inspire individuals to learn. Leaders must create a workplace environment that inspires individuals to want to learn — an environment in which creativity, curiosity, hope and sense-making are enabled and encouraged.
- Create structures for collaboration and teamwork. The

model also emphasizes two important relational components: belonging to a group that supports one's learning, and collaborating with others. Teamwork and collaboration is especially valuable with difficult or highly complex learning.

- Keep individuals engaged with others, while maintaining their independence. Openness to learning is about dependence on others, which involves moderation. Individuals should not be too dependent on others for their learning, and thus take no control or responsibility for the process; at the same time, they cannot close themselves off from others, and lose the benefit of collaboration or access to new perspectives, skills and knowledge. Leaders can help individuals find the right balance of openness to learning.

Learning ultimately succeeds when internal drive and openness to learning is reinforced by a collaborative, supportive environment.

REFERENCES

Developing Resilient Agency in Learning. *Ruth Deakin Crick, Shaofu Huang, Adeela Ahmed Shafi, Chris Goldspink. British Journal of Education Studies* **(April 3, 2015).**

Access this and more Ideas at **ideasforleaders.com**

HOW TO LIMIT AMBIGUITY OF RESPONSIBILITY AND LEARN FROM FAILURE

KEY CONCEPT

Failed experiences are not always a bad thing; they can be sources of learning, and improved performance. However, individuals do not always learn from failure. Whether they attribute that failure internally or externally has a role to play in their learning, and an additional factor is how ambiguous their responsibility for that task was. This Idea explores these factors and more.

IDEA SUMMARY

The nature and dynamics of today's organizations are such that failures are almost inevitable; the failure of a new product initiative or the failure of an existing strategy to meet changing organizational demands are common examples. Management and psychology research has focused on highlighting tools and resources designed to help people learn from failures, and such studies have traditionally suggested that those most able to learn from failed experiences will be those most likely to succeed in the future as well.

However, a study from Ross School of Business, Kenan-Flagler Business School and Harvard Business School has demonstrated that although individuals can learn from failed experiences, they do not always do so. Internal or external attributions occur after failure (or indeed any experience) that can impact an individual's learning from it.

Individuals are thought to typically attribute unsuccessful outcomes externally (i.e. to uncontrollable situational factors) in order to maintain a positive self-image. Some people, however, may be generally more inclined towards internal attribution. Both can alter how they engage in reflection and learning following that experience.

Through their empirical studies, the researchers found that when responsibility is more ambiguous, individuals are less likely to internally attribute their failures, and this greater external attribution undermines their efforts to learn and improve their performance. 'Ambiguity of responsibility' can be described as when characteristics of the task, such as its complexity or degree of accountability, and an individual's responsibility for performance are unclear.

Methodology: Christopher Myers, Bradley Staats and Francesca Gino conducted three studies to test their hypotheses. The first was a field study with Samasource, a non-profit data services firm, where they analyzed the work of 233 employees performing data-entry tasks over approximately eight months.

For the second study, they recruited professionals to take part in two decision-making activities, spaced one week apart. Finally, for the third study, the researchers recruited participants to take part in the trial of a new image-labelling tool to be used in the medical profession. The idea was that this task would be challenging and unfamiliar to participants, making it more likely that they would believe feedback indicating they had failed.

BUSINESS APPLICATION
What are the practical implications of these findings for managers and leaders in organizations? According to Myers, Staats and Gino, they should strive to actively manage perceptions of ambiguity of responsibility, as this may be the key factor that results in either internal or external attribution after failure; the former is more desirable to ensure

employees learn from failed experiences.

The use of after-event reviews (i.e. careful debriefing of a task experience) may be helpful, and has been highlighted by previous research as well. Myers, Staats and Gino add that organizations should also utilize strategies such as job design to help limit ambiguity of responsibility.

Managers should also be careful to not provide alternative explanations that heighten ambiguity of responsibility for a task; instead, they should focus their attention on what happened and how failure is an activity from which individuals and organizations can learn and improve with effort. Such feedback can allow individuals to develop a mindset of growing from failure, without introducing alternative explanations for the failed experience, such as excuses or scapegoats.

REFERENCES

"My Bad!" How Internal Attribution and Ambiguity of Responsibility Affect Learning from Failure. *Christopher G. Myers, Bradley R. Staats & Francesca Gino. Harvard Business School NOM Unit Working Paper No. 14-104* (April 2014).

Access this and more Ideas at **ideasforleaders.com**

What does a rave and your next team meeting have in common?

Host Leadership sees the leader adopt the habits and duties of a host of any gathering of people, creating the space and atmosphere, inviting people in, and setting the rules. They simultaneously serve guests and take the lead, and crucially they participate fully in the event.

Ideas for Leaders' new self-paced online program takes a deep dive into the context, thinking and impact of this essential leadership approach. **Comprising 24 short videos, quizzes and reflective questions**, the course is presented by **Dr Mark McKergow**, co-creator of the Host Leadership model and co-author of *Host Leadership: Six New Roles of Engagement*.

Enroll at our earlybird rate at programs.ideasforleaders.com

HOST LEADERSHIP

IDEAS FOR LEADERS
CHANGING THE WAY WE THINK

READING GROUP EMOTIONS IS KEY TO TRANSFORMATIONAL LEADERSHIP

KEY CONCEPT

Transformational leaders can pick up on cues from a group that convey its emotions — a skill that is beyond the individual-based emotional intelligence.

IDEA SUMMARY

Being aware and attending to the emotions of others is recognized as one of the key skills of today's transformational leaders — leaders who inspire and engage their people. However, when most leadership experts and researchers talk about a leader's 'people' or 'followers,' they are tacitly referring to individuals. In other words, the transformational leadership skills in question refer to the ability of a leader to 'read' the mood of individual people and respond accordingly — what is known in psychological terms as individual affect recognition, as it involves the ability to recognize affective cues displayed by individuals.

Sometimes, however, the one-on-one interactions required for individual affect recognition are not possible. A leader may be responsible for too large a group to be able to develop one-on-one relationships with individuals in the group.

Even more importantly, individual reactions may not always convey the mood of the group as a whole. For example, for a team that is not getting the resources it needs, there is a collective frustration that may not be reflected by just looking at the team members as individuals. In other words, transformational leaders also have to be able to 'read the group' — what is known as collective affect recognitio

Examples of collective affect recognition include a rock star who responds to a stadium of cheering fans or a police commander who gauges the growing restlessness of a crowd of protestors.

In previous research on collective affect recognition, Jeffrey Sanchez-Burks of University of Michigan's Ross School of Business and Quy Huy of Insead Singapore had introduced the concept of 'emotional aperture' or EA. By changing a camera's aperture setting, a photographer can either focus on an individual in the foreground or bring the entire scene into focus. Likewise, by shifting his or her emotional aperture, a leader can focus on one individual or on the entire group.

Making such an 'aperture' shift from individual affect recognition to collective affect recognition requires shifting from what psychologists call 'local' processing to 'global' processing. For example, a person sitting alone in a crowded coffee shop may just listen to the general noise around her — an example of global processing. Or she may focus on a specific conversation nearby — an example of local processing.

Global processing is not the accumulation of local processing. In other words, the person sitting in the coffee shop does not listen to each individual conversation and then aggregate them into a sense of the noise in the entire coffee shop. Instead, local processing and global processing are two distinct psychological processes.

This distinction creates a challenge for the research of collective affect recognition: you cannot test the ability to process globally with the same methodology that you use to test the ability to process locally. You need a distinct test. However, in the past affect recognition tests have been based on individual affect recognition. No separate test existed that was specifically designed to assess the ability for collective affect recognition.

To resolve this challenge, Sanchez-Burks and Huy, working with Caroline Bartel of the University of Texas McComb School of Business and Laura Rees of Vanderbilt's Owen Graduate School of Management, developed a new measurement tool specifically designed to measure the ability to recognize collective affect. The new tool is called the Emotional Aperture Measure or EAM.

The EAM was built from a database of facial images that the research team manipulated, through Photoshop, to create a series of images. Each image showed groups of people from various ethnicities displaying a variety of emotions. The researchers created short videos so that the images would appear and quickly disappear — recreating the effect of seeing a crowd of people and gauging from visual cues the 'mood' of the crowd. Scoring the EAM was based on a scale of 0-2 points for each movie: 2 points if the leader watching the movie gave the correct number of people with positive and negative emotions; 1 point if the participant only gave the correct number for only one of the emotions (negative or positive); 0 points if the participant failed to give the correct number of people with either emotion.

To test the validity of their new measurement tool, the research team created an experiment in which participants were primed to either think locally or globally. After first completing the EAM, participants in the experiment examined an abstract painting by Jackson Pollock. Participants were instructed to focus on the painting as a whole (global priming) or one aspect of the painting (local priming). The participants then completed the EAM a second time. The results showed that participants primed to think globally scored much higher on the EAM than those primed to think locally. The EAM accurately reflected the ability for collective affect recognition.

In a second experiment, the research team used the EAM to confirm the distinction between recognizing affective cues by individuals and recognizing affective cues by groups. Combining the EAM with tests that measured individual affect recognition, the team found little correlation between those who were skilled at recognizing affective cues in a group and those skilled at recognizing affective cues in individuals.

A third experiment was particularly instructive: it tested whether there was a correlation between collective affect recognition and transformational leadership skills. The research team surveyed 91 top managers and nearly 900 of their subordinates (an average of about 9 subordinates per manager). The results were unequivocal: managers who scored high on the EAM also scored high in the view of their subordinates on transformational leadership skills. No such significant correlation existed between individual affect recognition and transformational leadership..

BUSINESS APPLICATION
A leader's ability to read the mood and mindset of a group is obviously a key ingredient for effective leadership, from

dealing with a specific situation or incident to developing the type of open mutually respectful relationship with the group at the foundation of inspiring transformational leadership. One specific example of the power of collective affect recognition is related to leading significant change. Group dynamics can often play a significant role in your team's or employees' response to change. It is not enough to gauge the response of individuals; you must gauge the response of the group as a whole, which will allow you to choose the most effective group-level strategies for acquiring buy-in and engagement.

In sum, the core lessons of this research — 1) that the ability to read the emotions of individuals does not mean you are equally adept at reading the emotions of the group, and 2) that for transformational leadership, recognizing affective cues in the group is more important than individual cues — can help leaders focus on their relationship goals with their groups, and diagnose leadership issues that may be at the root of some of their challenges (e.g., resistance to change).

REFERENCES

Assessing Collective Affect Recognition via the Emotional Aperture Measure. *Jeffrey Sanchez-Burks, Caroline Bartel, Laura Rees & Quy Huy. Cognition and Emotion* (2016).

Access this and more Ideas at **ideasforleaders.com**

Book Reviews

A New Way to Think

Your Guide to Superior
Management Effectiveness

By Roger L Martin

*Published by Harvard Business Review Press, May
2022, 256 pages, ISBN 978-1-647-82351-1*

Energy price hikes, soaring inflation and the war in Ukraine
have made the post-pandemic 'build back better' task harder
than ever—but hugely necessary.

'Better' suggests a greater focus on social justice and
environmental responsibility, but with the rising cost of living
disproportionately effecting poorer people and developing
countries, and the energy crisis likely to de-rail the 'net-zero'
climate change agenda, maintaining the status quo will be difficult—better extremely hard.

Written during the Covid crisis, but before the war in
Europe, Roger L. Martin's latest book, *A New Way to Think: A
Guide to Superior Management Effectiveness,* offers valuable
direction for organizations facing the daunting task ahead.
Martin's central message is that business leaders get too hung
up on their business models—typically repeating the same

model with greater energy even if it initially fails.

In order to set new trajectories for sustainable growth, leaders need to 'own' their models and not be dictated to by them. If the model—"a given framework, general practice, theory, or way of thinking"—isn't working it should be ditched and replaced.

Across fourteen concise chapters, Martin, Professor Emeritus and former Dean of Rotman School of Management, University of Toronto, examines fourteen dominant but flawed business models from every area of management and in each case offers a new way of thinking to find a better model. The message is that leaders should stop blaming themselves when their model fails them—it's likely to be the fault of the model not their fault in poorly implementing it. Try a different model.

These are the areas he focuses on: *competition; stakeholders; customers; strategy; data; culture; knowledge work; corporate functions; planning; execution; talent; innovation; capital investment; and M&A.*

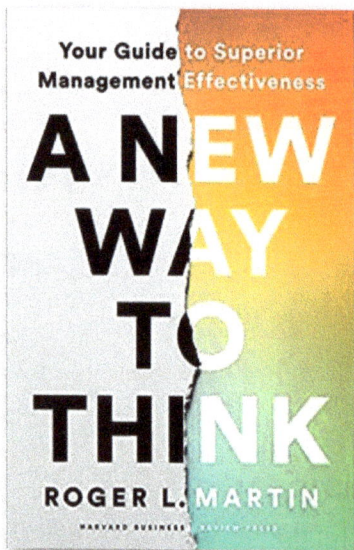

Of 'competition' he says that it happens on the customer-facing front line rather than at corporate HQ—the traditional hierarchy is flipped and the role at each level should be to help the level below to serve the customer better.

When, in a recent report, EY posited that "big data can eliminate reliance on 'gut feel' decision making," they exposed another dominant model that Martin says is faulty. Here he argues that in a context where things *cannot be other than they are* data-analytics is valuable in improving performance. But where things *need to be other than they are* reliance on data can inadvertently convince us that change is not possible.

With execution Martin contests the dominant idea that "a mediocre idea well executed is superior to a great idea poorly executed." He argues that this model can indefinitely consign the organization to mediocrity. Unfortunately, in this case he concedes that his new model may find few takers, as the flawed but dominant model does enshrine an important principle to ensure action orientation. His hope is however that readers will open their minds to each of his fourteen models—even giving the execution one a chance.

Considered one of the foremost management thinkers of his generation, Professor Martin has previously written about some of the major structural problems in democratic capitalism—the disconnect between Main Street and Wall Street, the dynamics of social enterprise, etc. This book is something of a return to basics, to providing sound applicable advice to management practitioners, and as such, drawing on his unique depth of experience and ever creative mind, it is an important contribution.

Curious Minds

The Power of Connection

By Perry Zurn and Dani S Bassett

Published by MIT Press, September 2022, 304 pages, ISBN: 978-0262047036

Books on curiosity proliferate, not at least because of its importance in the context of leadership and organization. However, most if not all books about the subject stick to a 2000-year-old paradigm that relates curiosity to an individual's desire to learn, to find out, to acquire new knowledge.

Curious Minds: The Power of Connection is refreshingly different. It radically reframes the elusive concept of curiosity in a way that elevates it to a new epistemological level.

The authors – Perry Zurn and Dani S. Bassett – are identical twins who are themselves deeply curious, one (Perry) as a philosopher and critical theorist, the other (Dani) as a bioengineer and neuroscientist. Intellectually and aesthetically deeply satisfying, they travel between the realms of art, neuroscience,

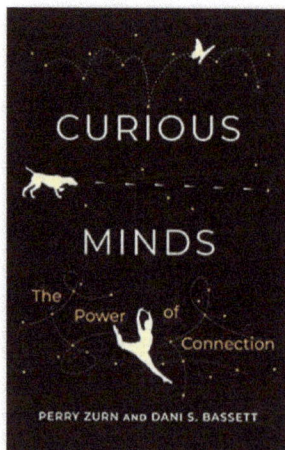

history, philosophy, literature, psychology, sociology - you name it - shining an intriguing light on a subject that gets usually seen only through the narrow lens of a single discipline.

What I love most – apart from the beautiful, almost poetic writing - is that, oscillating between neural and sociological network theory, they reveal the essence of curiosity as a *connectivity* practice.

Here is one highlight of many: The authors distinguish three archetypes of curious minds: *Busybodies* are curious about everything, no matter if is relevant for their immediate context. They build horizontal knowledge (and relationships) across a wide area of subjects – but without much depth. *Hunters*, on the other hand, go rather deep than wide. They dig into a distinctive subject matter and want to know everything about it. They build vertical knowledge – but without much breadth. And then there are *Dancers*, a type of curiosity that thrives on disruption and on breaking the mold. As Perry Zurn beautifully puts it: *"Dancers query on the wings of inspiration, nonplussed by the lack of guardrails or precedents, and ready to take risks."*

You can tell between the lines that the authors have a lot of sympathy for this third type - the "Dancer" - and so do I. After all, this type of curious behaviour is closest related to creativity and courage, to entrepreneurship, to the urge to conquer unknown spaces. While the aimless curious roaming of busybodies may lead at times to creative inspiration and unexpected discoveries, it tends to remain on the surface and lack contextualization, reminiscent of Jacks of all Trades, who – taken to the extreme - know everything about nothing. And while the focused curiosity of hunters may lead them to unique insights and expertise, they remain in a narrow silo, lacking connectivity across horizontal knowledge boundaries, reminiscent of experts who – taken to the extreme - know everything about nothing.

Dancing, on the other hand, thrives as much on the horizontal as it does on the vertical. Not unlike hunters, dancers are driven by a purpose of discovery, but they discover by constantly crossing boundaries, digging deeper at times, but moving on to connect their learnings with unfamiliar contexts – connections which in turn create new pathways in their cognitive maps.

Connection is the keyword here, and it runs like a red thread through the book. What makes the reading experience so unique, is that the authors come from epistemological highly diverse backgrounds – yet they are deeply connected as identical twins who grew up together. The interplay of palpable connectivity and deep scholarly diversity results in a creative and developmental tension between the 8 chapters of the book, which alternate like a pendulum between neuroscience and philosophy, feeding off each other like a ping-pong game as the thread of argument unwinds. In other words – we as readers become witnesses of the authors' curious "dance" that unfolds in front of our eyes.

Curiosity as a driver that creates social texture, constituting and feeding relationship networks on the individual, organizational, and societal level. That's a very welcome novel view, with significant implications for leadership, organization, and ecosystems. An enlightening and inspiring read.

Fortitude

Unlocking the Secrets of Inner Strength

By Bruce Daisley

Published by Cornerstone Press, August 2022, 336 pages, ISBN: 978-1-847-94365-1

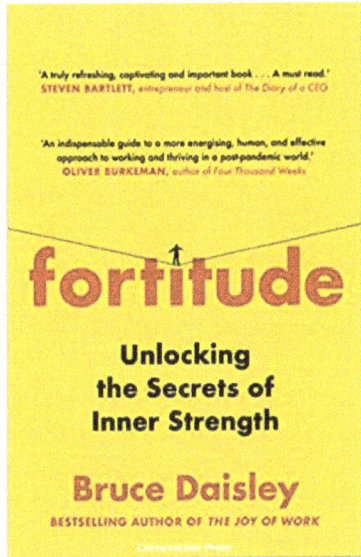

Resilience is a quality that has been sustaining humanity for millennia, but has become very much in vogue in the last half decade, and even more so since the pandemic forced us all to battle a bit harder in adversity.

Bruce Daisley, formerly Twitter's top man in Europe and the best-selling author of The Joy of Work, burrows through the research on resilience to create this entertaining insight into what makes some people resilient and others fall-by-the-wayside as the slings and arrows of outrageous fortune are hurled in our direction.

His opening premise explores the Great British Medallist research undertaken before the 2012 London Olympic Games to identify what makes winners and discovered that of the 16

Super-elite athletes studied (those who had won gold medals at top events) all had had some form of childhood traumatic event, while the 16 Elite athletes, (those who made it to world-class competition but didn't win) saw only 4 out of 12 have such experiences.

Had traumatic events (death of parents, divorce, abuse or other) played a part in developing the elite mindset and that will-to-win over all else? A wider survey shows that, unsurprisingly, many traumatized children have their lives devastated by these events. There is clearly more to it than just seeing who copes with trauma well.

Daisley unpacks a huge archive of psychological research in the book, and brings in a spectrum of stories of soldiers, teachers, medics and family relationships, to construct his Three Pillars of Fortitude, which parallel David McClelland's of the 1950s (Power; Achievement; Affiliation) and psychologists Richard Ryan and Edward Deci's 'Self-Determination Theory' of the 1990s (Autonomy; Competence; Relatedness) to come up with his own triptych of: Control; Identity; Community.

The ability to have Control over our own actions and within the group is fundamental to our ability to prosper and thrive. What Daisley highlights is that control tends to come with status, the more status the more control we have, and the inverse is weakening for those lower down the ladder.

The second pillar, Identity, plays a central role in the way sport enables athletes to recover from trauma – they reimagine their identities, not as someone who has suffered abuse, but by someone who wins. This insight plays across us all – if we have a clear self-identity and live to that, fulfilling that role, then we tend to be happier and more confident in what we are doing. Uncertainty over what we are doing is under-mining.

The final strand is Community. Daisley spends a lot of time on this, teasing apart how our sense of our 'ingroup' and what we make of the 'outgroups' effects our behaviours. Illustrating the 'bounce back' exhibited by survivors of collective trauma, such as the London Blitz or 9/11, those that can recover together, tend to do better than those who are isolated. He mentions Emile Durkheim's phrase of 'collective effervescence' to encompass this state; and suggests that the disappearance of our Neanderthal ancestors by Sapiens, was not so much that Neanderthals were stupid (he posits that their larger skull sizes indicate they may have been cleverer) but by the fact that Sapiens were more sociable, and that collective strength overcame the more individualistic culture of Neanderthals. Something for the Anglo-Saxon west to ponder perhaps!

Whether Daisley's model is intrinsically better than McClelland's or Self-Determination Theory (and a host of others) is moot. What this book does excellently is pull together a wide range of interconnecting research to highlight that organizations need to seriously rethink how they design themselves. Currently most are designed so as to limit individual agency (control), individual's sense of purpose (identity) is rarely brought into focus – and we have so little time in today's work environment to stop and bond with colleagues, so that community is hugely fractured, if it exists at all.

There is much to learn from Fortitude in the search for making organizations more human – and sustainably productive.

Uncommon Accountability

A Radical New Approach to Greater Success and Fulfillment

By Brian P. Moran and Michael Lennington

Published by Wiley, March 2022, 208 pages, ISBN 978-1-11976-492-2

Words matter. 'Accountability'—in the sense of taking ownership and responsibility for our actions—should be a guiding principle for all human endeavour and certainly for all aspects of leadership.

Unfortunately, this weighty word has been misappropriated, and is now only ever seen in a negative light—applying to misdeeds but not to their opposite. While we say a football manager should be 'held accountable' for losses, when the team is riding high, we do not say he or she should be 'held accountable' for

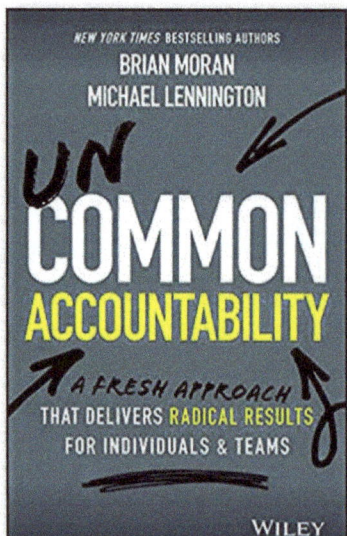

the success. The OED defines 'accountable' as: i) responsible for someone or some action; answerable. ii) able to be explained. Nothing bad is implied. Yet being 'called to account' has a very negative ring.

In their new book, *Uncommon Accountability*, Brian P. Moran and Michael Lennington, principals at the change management consultancy The Execution Company, look at the true meaning of this important word, arguing that ownership of one›s choices and the discipline to act effectively on these choices is at the heart of accountability. Whether the result of any action is a success or a failure is not the point. The danger with the word used, as it typically is, in a negative sense is that it discourages productive actions by causing undue wariness, low self-belief and a lack of trust that we can achieve our goals. It promotes a fear of failure.

Though the book is subtitled 'A Radical New Approach to Greater Success and Fulfillment', it is perhaps not so much 'new' as a return to the old original understanding of accountability that can bring these greater qualities. The core message presented here is that applied in its fullest sense accountability—for good and bad—can be a prime motivator and driver of human enterprise and an essential characteristic of good leadership. And that establishing accountability in its true sense in teams and across organizations has the potential to lift employee engagement and transform performance.

At its core the book emphasizes the vital importance of personal choice in every interaction. It accentuates the positive aspect of accountability and explains how it can be used to foster a growth and learning mindset, while discouraging feelings of victimhood, stress and negativity. It shows how individuals and teams that take ownership of their decisions, actions and roles can outperform those that have a traditional employee mindset, stating that: "Employees work to the core job description; owners work to deliver their best results and live the mission."

The authors consider the concept of behavioural consequences—looking at positive and negative reinforcement, punishment and penalty—and show how best to manage negative consequences by "holding others capable" and avoiding the blame game. A leader that manages by citing consequences is likely to only get the minimum effort form their team—or themselves. The focus should instead be on ensuring everyone is encouraged and supported to achieve what they are 'capable' of. Consequences, they argue, are not bad—they help shape behaviour—but crucially: "consequences are not, and never will be, 'accountability'."

Rich in real-world case studies, that explore the principles of Uncommon Accountability put into practice, the book takes what appears to be a simple idea and develops it into a surprisingly comprehensive tool for unlocking personal and team potential and driving performance.

The Medium.
The Message.

Accessible new format. Accessible new leadership insights, developments and learning. Subscribe to the printed edition for big ideas in your back pocket.

About the Publishers

Ideas for Leaders

Ideas for Leaders summarizes the thinking of the foremost researchers and experts on leadership and management practice from the world's top business schools and management research institutions. With these concise and easily readable 'Ideas' you can quickly and easily inform yourself and your colleagues about the latest insights into management best practice.

The research-based Ideas are supported by a growing series of podcasts with influential thinkers, CEOs, and other leading leadership and management experts from large organizations and small. We also publish book reviews and a new series of online programs.

www.ideasforleaders.com

The Center for the Future of Organization (CFFO)

CFFO is an independent Think Tank and Research Center at the Drucker School of Management at Claremont Graduate University. The Center's mission is to deepen our understanding of new capabilities that are critical to succeed in a digitally connected world, and to support leaders and organizations along their transformational journey.

In the tradition of Peter Drucker, the Center works across disciplines, combining conceptual depth with practical applicability and ethical responsibility, in close collaboration and connection with thought leaders and practice leaders from academia, business, and consulting.

www.futureorg.org

DLQ Advisory Board

DevelopingLeaders Quarterly

www.ingramcontent.com/pod-product-compliance
Lightning Source LLC
Chambersburg PA
CBHW040932210326
41597CB00030B/5274